A LITTLE BIT

OF

WICCA

A LITTLE BIT

OF

WICCA

AN INTRODUCTION TO WITCHCRAFT

CASSANDRA EASON

STERLING ETHOS
New York

STERLING ETHOS
New York

An Imprint of Sterling Publishing
1166 Avenue of the Americas
New York, NY 10036

Text © 2017 Cassandra Eason

ISBN 978-1-4549-2712-9

Distributed in Canada by Sterling Publishing Co., Inc.
c/o Canadian Manda Group, 664 Annette Street
Toronto, Ontario, Canada M6S 2C8
Distributed in the United Kingdom by GMC Distribution Services
Castle Place, 166 High Street, Lewes, East Sussex, England BN7 1XU
Distributed in Australia by NewSouth Books
45 Beach Street, Coogee, NSW 2034, Australia

For information about custom editions, special sales, and premium and corporate purchases, please
contact Sterling Special Sales at 800-805-5489 or specialsales@sterlingpublishing.com.

Manufactured in the United States of America

4 6 8 10 9 7 5
sterlingpublishing.com

Image Credits: **iStock:** © Del_Mar: 109-114; © PeterHermesFurian: 16; **Britt Sabo:** 82;
Shutterstock: © Verpeya: throughout (pentagram)

CONTENTS

INTRODUCTION

WHAT IS WICCA, ITS ORIGINS, AND HOW THE MAGICK WORKS

WICCA, THE CRAFT OF THE WISE, IS THE PRACTICAL EXPRESSION OF the spiritual and belief system of those who work seriously and reverently with magick. It is centered on the conscious and responsible use of natural, cosmic, and personal psychic powers to move thoughts into actuality through the raising, amplifying, concentration, and release of these energies. Wicca is also the name of the major organized religion of neo (or new) pagan witchcraft, which is based on ancient magickal practices. Gerald Gardner formed the first formally established neo pagan worship group in the years after the repeal of the Witchcraft Act in 1951 in the UK, though of course there were hereditary witches in America, Europe, and indeed throughout the settled world. Pagan, which comes from the Roman word *paganus*, or country dweller, refers to natural forms of spirituality, both organized and personal, of those who follow the cycles of the year and the seasons, as Wiccans do.

In the home, the family matriarch throughout the centuries and in many cultures had secret recipes, remedies, and folk customs, which were passed down orally through the generations, as well as rituals and charms to bring love, prosperity, fertility, healing, and protection to the family members and the home. Many older people in Scandinavia and Europe and those of Scandinavian and Eastern or Western European descent in the Americas, Australia, New Zealand, and South Africa can still recall their great grandmothers carrying out such magick as part of the family folk custom. There are many variations of Wicca, and some witches do not call themselves Wiccans. Some Wiccans work primarily as healers and ecologists rather than magickal practitioners.

A Little Bit of Wicca is a comprehensive guide to practicing Wicca, whether you are a total beginner or are already on the path and wish to learn more about the methods and structure of Wicca.

WHO ARE WICCANS?

Wicca can be defined as the craft of those who seek, and hopefully attain, wisdom and create or carry out ceremonies to celebrate and give energies to the rising and falling year.

There is a vast amount of information now available about

Wiccan practices and about its complex but fascinating origins that helps to show the richness and beauty of the tradition. This information also depicts the great suffering that witches in past centuries have experienced in order to keep Wiccan traditions alive and evolving. Above all, Wicca is not set in stone but is constantly changing through the wisdom and experiences of every witch who contributes fresh insights. And so, having studied the basic structure, you are free to, and indeed should, create your own unique path.

Wiccans may be Christian, Buddhist, belong to any other religion, or belong to none, but all positively recognize a higher and eternal source of goodness and light.

WHAT IS MAGICK?

Magick is a natural energy that is part of the flowing life force that, like any energy, is essentially neutral, which is the reason high ethics must be such an integral part of Wicca and magick generally. By creating chants, specific spells, and more openly structured rituals, we can transform and manifest our positive thoughts and wishes into actuality.

The natural world, even in more formal rituals, acts as a powerhouse of magickal energy that can be used to amplify our personal psychic powers. We can tap into specific times of the day, week, or month and into the ever-changing energies of the sun, moon, seas, lakes, rivers, weather, flowers, herbs, trees, and crystals.

If you ask for something through magick, you should always give a little kindness or encouragement in return to a person, animal, or place in need. That way the positive energies and resources are recycled.

DEDICATING YOURSELF TO THE MAGICKAL PATH

Dedication is the term used for a conscious commitment to the Craft and can be made when you begin magick and/or at any time on your path when you may want to remind yourself of your magickal quest.

Once it was said that only a witch could make another witch, and I respect those who believe that. But increasingly, solitary witches do wish to ceremonially mark their own initial, spiritual commitment to the Wiccan craft and acknowledge the positive spiritual change that working with witchcraft brings within the practitioner.

If you are establishing a coven, you can, each of you, carry out this ritual at the same time in a circle of trees, moving at your own pace, and when you have finished, sit silently and wait until all are seated against their chosen tree. Then rise together and say, in unison, *We are the coven of the wise; may we always work in beauty and in sanctity as the [state your new coven name if you have chosen it]. So shall it be.*

If you have not already done so, choose a name by which you will be known in the Wiccan craf—perhaps a favorite deity, a power animal, or a tree or crystal that has magickal significance for you. Some practitioners use this name in the presence of other witches and speak it aloud when practicing magick. But others believe this name must never be spoken, or even written, as you then give others power over you. This is entirely your choice. It is also often said that this is the name you rediscover from past worlds, where you have previously trodden the path of the wise.

In Chapter 1 we will set up a Wiccan altar
and collect and dedicate your magickal tools.

THE WICCAN ALTAR AND MAGICKAL TOOLS

THE ALTAR IS HEART OF ANY WITCH'S LIFE. EVEN IF YOU belong to a en or group of witches, you will still want your own spal sacred place at home, as well as a communal one.

WHAT IS AN ALTAR?

It is any table or fl supported surface on which you arrange and display your special magickal tools, crystals, statues, and spell or ritual ingredients, and that is used as a focus for your spells and rituals.

Altars can be circular, square, or rectangular. Generally, an altar is positioned in the northern part of a room or area, though some traditions use the east.

Choose a cloth for your altar, perhaps embroidered or of silk. You can again vary it according to the seasons and change the color as appropriate to the ritual.

...miture ...will need ceremo-
...or ormal... Use a compass or
...our alt.make the directional
...nt point and the altar.

I will mark with an asterisk the essentir any altar for Wiccan
rituals. You can include the ret as is apprte for your practice.

THE SUBSTANCES AND MATERIALS THAT MAJP RITUAL

***One or two central altar candles in whit ream, or natural
beeswax.** From the central altar candle(s), will light all the other
candles used in the ritual. If you begin wit ro candles, place them
centrally but a little farther to the right and t on the altar than if
you use a single candle. In my tradition, I p the Goddess candle
on the left and the God candle on the right he two candles
represent the Goddess and God energies, re tively. If only using
one candle, it signifies the God and Goddes ergies united.)

God and Goddess representations. For balanc these I reverse
from where I placed the central candles, with m God statue on the
left and the Goddess statue within the central c dles. But again, it
is your choice. You can use statues from any cult re and can, if you
wish, mix the cultures. You can also use a large c nchlike shell for
the Goddess and a bone horn or small antler for the God. (C nch is
a tropical marine mollusk with a robust spiral shell.)

**Four elemental candles in appropriate color set at your direc-
tional marker points.** The colors are: g en or brown for the north
and Earth; yellow, purple, or gray f r the east and Air; red, orange, or
gold for the south and Fire; nd blue or silver for the west and Water.

T HE ALTAR IS THE HEART OF ANY WITCH'S LIFE. EVEN IF YOU belong to a coven or group of witches, you will still want your own special sacred place at home, as well as a communal one.

WHAT IS AN ALTAR?

It is any table or flat supported surface on which you arrange and display your special magickal tools, crystals, statues, and spell or ritual ingredients, and that is used as a focus for your spells and rituals.

Altars can be circular, square, or rectangular. Generally, an altar is positioned in the northern part of a room or area, though some traditions use the east.

Choose a cloth for your altar, perhaps embroidered or of silk. You can again vary it according to the seasons and change the color as appropriate to the ritual.

Setting an Altar with Magickal Tools and Materials

Whether you use a full-size or miniature altar, you will need ceremonial tools and materials for more formal magick. Use a compass or assess approximate directions on your altar and make the directional markers halfway at four equidistant points around the altar.

I will mark with an asterisk the essentials for any altar for Wiccan rituals. You can include the rest as is appropriate for your practice.

THE SUBSTANCES AND MATERIALS THAT MAKE UP RITUAL

*One or two central altar candles in white, cream, or natural beeswax. From the central altar candle(s), you will light all the other candles used in the ritual. If you begin with two candles, place them centrally but a little farther to the right and left on the altar than if you use a single candle. In my tradition, I place the Goddess candle on the left and the God candle on the right. (The two candles represent the Goddess and God energies, respectively. If only using one candle, it signifies the God and Goddess energies united.)

God and Goddess representations. For balance, these I reverse from where I placed the central candles, with my God statue on the left and the Goddess statue within the central candles. But again, it is your choice. You can use statues from any culture and can, if you wish, mix the cultures. You can also use a large conchlike shell for the Goddess and a bone horn or small antler for the God. (Conch is a tropical marine mollusk with a robust spiral shell.)

Four elemental candles in appropriate colors set at your directional marker points. The colors are: green or brown for the north and Earth; yellow, purple, or gray for the east and Air; red, orange, or gold for the south and Fire; and blue or silver for the west and Water.

Alternatively, you can set these elemental candles around the perimeter of any circle you cast or in the center of each of the four walls of the room in which you are working. If you are casting a simple spell, you would use just the four elemental substances listed below on your altar plus a symbol or offerings dish in the center and, if you wish, a single central candle to represent God and Goddess energies combined.

*A dish of salt representing Earth will be in the north of the altar.

*Incense (a cone, stick, or a dish of non-combustible incense powder or granules) burned on a dish of charcoal in the east for Air.

*A candle in red, orange, or gold, or, if you are using elemental candles as well, pure-white for the Fire element in the south.

*A bowl of water or rose or lavender fragrance in the west for Water.

WICCAN MAGICKAL TOOLS

I have listed first the four essential tools traditionally used in more formal Wiccan rituals, noted with an asterisk. The others can add to a ritual but are not as necessary.

*Athame/Knife

This is set in the eastern corner of the altar, to the right of the incense, and represents the element of Air.

Athames are traditionally double-edged and black-handled, but a single-edged blade is safer (some Wiccan traditions begin the ritual in the east and not the north, and so use the athame for Fire in the south). However, the blade that corresponds with the tarot suit of Air seems to me most natural in the east.

You can obtain an athame from a specialist magickal shop or online. Alternatively, buy an ornamental knife in souvenir stores or in antique or hunting equipment shops, or you can simply use a carved silver paper knife. The latter is ideal for a miniature altar.

Sword

The sword is a more elaborate form of the athame and is usually reserved for larger-scale indoor or outdoor ceremonies. Like the athame, the sword is placed in the east (or in the alternative tradition, the south) of the altar, to the right of the incense (the left if you have the athame as well). It is a tool of the Air element if set in the east.

Swords can be used for drawing magickal circles on a forest floor, in the earth, or in snow (my favorite). They can also be used for greeting the Guardians—the traditional protectors of the four directions—in formal rituals. The Guardians are often regarded as four Archangels, four deities, four Power animals, or as the Elemental Spirits, who signify the four forces: Earth, Air, Water, and Fire.

You can easily obtain reproduction ceremonial swords that are not sharp. Military museums may sell ornate ones.

*Chalice

The chalice or ritual goblet represents the Water element and is placed in the west of the altar, to the right of the bowl of water. On a smaller altar, it can be used to contain the water instead of a bowl.

The knife, sword, or wand is ceremonially plunged into the chalice as a symbolic union of the God and Goddess energies, which is the climax of a ritual (especially love rituals).

The chalice is also central to the sacred cakes and ale rite that occurs at the end of very formal ceremonies and is in this case filled with red wine or fruit juice that is blessed and passed around the group to drink, or carried around by the High Priestess (who represents Goddess energies) for everyone to drink. The chalice is traditionally made of silver, but you can also use crystal glass, stainless steel, or pewter. This corresponds with the Water suit in the tarot.

*Pentacle/Pentagram

The pentacle—a pentagram or five-pointed star enclosed within a circle—is a symbol of the Earth and is placed in the north of the altar.

The pentacle may be found as a freestanding item but is more usually painted on a flat round dish or disc. The pentagram itself is protective or empowering, depending on which way it is drawn, and has many uses in ritual.

You can buy a pentacle dish made of metal, wood, or pottery from a New Age store, or paint or etch your own pentagram/pentacle on a plain glass or ceramic dish. If you prefer you can trace an invisible invoking or attracting pentagram on any plain dish with the index finger of the hand you write with each time before use (see page 56 for an example of an invoking or attracting pentagram).

This corresponds with the Earth tarot suit of pentacles or coins.

*Wand

The wand is a symbol of Fire in many traditions and should be placed in the south of the altar, to the right of the candle. Wands can be obtained from New Age stores or online, but if possible, try to handle a wand before buying it in order to make sure you're choosing the one that's right for you. Alternately, you can use a long, clear quartz crystal, pointed at one end and rounded at the other, as a wand.

While wands are traditionally made of wood, they can also be made of metal, and especially copper. However, if you don't find the right wand in stores or online, you can easily make your own. The wand is used for enchanting or filling a symbol with power in a spell or ritual by making circles over a symbol (clockwise for attracting energies and counter-clockwise for banishing energies). It can also be used for raising and releasing magickal power.

Bell

The bell stands in the north of the circle, to the right of the salt, and is an Earth symbol. Use a silver- or gold-colored bell or a Tibetan pair of bells you can strike together. The bell is often rung nine times at the beginning and end of each ritual while standing in the south of the circle, facing north, or at each of the four directional points to call the Guardians.

Cauldron

This is a three-legged iron pot. It is one of the most versatile items of magick since it can be set in the center of a large space indoors or outdoors or in its true elemental position in the north. In less-formal rituals, it can sometimes form the central focus of a ritual instead of an altar, and this works especially effectively outdoors.

Cauldrons can be bought in New Age stores, by mail order, or from antique markets. If you look around cookware or even gardening centers you may find your cauldron under a different name.

PURIFYING AND EMPOWERING CEREMONIAL TOOLS AND THE ALTAR

The first time you use an altar, you should dedicate it. This ritual will also empower your magickal tools if you set them ready in their positions on the altar before beginning the ritual. Thereafter, whenever you get a new tool, you can set it in the center of the altar and it will be empowered during any formal ritual you carry out.

Step 1: Preparing the Altar

Make sure you have your tools and materials set in their places on the altar. The only addition is the bowl of perfume. Put it in the south of the altar. For perfume purification, use any cologne, such as sandalwood, rose, or lavender, or rose or lavender water.

Step 2: Beginning the Ritual

Ring the bell in each of the four Quarters—the four main directions—from north going clockwise and then return it to its place.

Light the altar candle(s) left to right and then the elemental candle in the south, saying for each: *May light illumine and fire purify this altar. I dedicate this altar and my work to the highest good and the purest intention.*

Now move the salt and water bowls so they are side-by-side in front of the altar candles, with the salt to the left.

Make a cross on the surface of the salt, either an equal-armed or Earth Mother diagonal cross, with a silver-colored knife or an athame, asking the blessing of the angels, the Goddess and God, or a favorite deity on the salt and the ritual.

Now stir the water three times clockwise with the same knife, again asking the blessing of the angels, the Goddess and God, or a favorite deity on the water and the ritual.

Take three pinches of salt and add to the water, swirling the bowl thrice clockwise, thrice counter-clockwise, and thrice clockwise, again asking the blessing of the angels, the Goddess and God, or a favorite deity on the now-sacred salt water and the ritual.

Sprinkle a few drops of sacred salt water in each of the four directions on the altar, saying before you begin: *May the power of the earth and waters empower and purify this altar. I dedicate this altar and my work to the highest good and the purest intention.*

Now sprinkle a little sacred salt water over each of the tools, going clockwise around the altar, saying: *May the power of the earth and waters empower and purify this tool, [name it]. I dedicate this altar and my work to the highest good and the purest intention.*

Next, take the incense and light it from each of the candles, or sprinkle your granular incense on preprepared and now-glowing white-hot charcoal in the dish.

Beginning in the east and moving clockwise, make smoke spirals over the four main direction points of the altar, wafting it with your hand or a feather if you are using granular incense or incense cones, saying before you begin: *May the power of the sky empower and purify this altar. I dedicate this altar and my work to the highest good and the purest intention.*

Waft it next over each tool in turn clockwise, saying: *May the power of the earth and waters empower and purify this tool, [name it]. I dedicate this altar and my work to the highest good and the purest intention.*

Next take the perfume bowl and, beginning in the south and moving clockwise, sprinkle a few drops of perfume in each of the four directions on the altar, saying before you begin: *May the power of this fragrance empower and purify this altar. I dedicate this altar and my work to the highest good and the purest intention.*

Sprinkle perfume over each tool in turn, again moving clockwise, saying: *May the power of the earth and waters empower and purify this tool, [name it]. I dedicate this altar and my work to the highest good and the purest intention.*

When you are ready, blow out first the Goddess candle, then the God candle, then the Fire element candle in the south, which will spread the light around the altar and into the tools and yourself, saying as you do: *So may my altar and my magickal tools be blessed. I dedicate them and myself to the greatest good and with the highest intent, healing all and harming none. So shall it be.*

Ring the bell in each direction, starting this time in the west and moving counter-clockwise to end in the north and return it to its place. Then say softly: *May blessings grow. It shall be so. So ends this rite.*

Sit quietly in the darkness, inhaling the residual fragrance, and anoint your main inner energy points—the center of your hairline, your brow, the base of your throat, and your two inner wrist points—with drops of perfume from the dish. Say: [at the hairline] *Above me the light,* [at the brow] *within me the fragrance,* [at the throat] *that I may speak truly* [at each wrist point] *the love in my heart.*

Leave the incense to burn and thank any deity or angel to whom you dedicated the rite along with your altar and tools.

If possible, leave everything in place for twenty-four hours and then wash the salt, water, perfume, and salt water away under a running tap and tidy everything away.

Step 3: Cleansing Your Magickal Tools and the Altar After a Ritual

Spiral a clear crystal pendulum over each tool and then over the four main directions of the altar and the center, making nine counter-clockwise circles over each one.

Plunge the pendulum in cold running water to cleanse it, and shake dry. Move the pendulum nine times clockwise, this time first over each artifact, the four directions of the altar, and the center of the altar again, to restore energies.

Wash the pendulum under running water.

In the next chapter, we will learn how to cast a Wiccan magickal circle.

CREATING THE MAGICK CIRCLE IN WICCA

A CIRCLE, WHETHER PHYSICALLY DRAWN OR SYMBOLICALLY created, marks an Otherworld place within which the restrictions of time and space do not apply. Here the four elements combine to create the energy and magickal substance Aether, or Akasha, in which thoughts can be transformed into actuality in the material world.

Also coming together within the circle are deities; angels; the four elemental Guardians of the directional Watchtowers, as the four directional marker points of the circle are called; the wise ancestors; and nature essences in outdoor rituals. The circle becomes a sacred extension of the altar space.

As a place of power, the circle excludes any negative energy from the everyday sphere. Because you are working with spiritual powers, it also prevents anything less than benign entering the sacred space, where you are spiritually open and vulnerable.

PREPARING FOR CIRCLE-CASTING

If you are carrying out a formal ritual, you may wish to bathe, adding salt or essential oils to your bath, and put on a special loose robe specifically for ritual, or, if you are in a hurry, anoint your higher four energy centers using fragrance as I described at the end of the previous chapter (page 10).

If the ritual uses smudge in the way described in the previous chapter, you should physically and psychically cleanse the circle area beforehand. You may wish to do this *before* bathing or anointing your chakras with fragrance or essential oil.

Alternatively, sweep or asperge (sprinkle with water and a small branch) where you will cast your circle. Keep a special broom, perhaps a traditional besom, for this purpose. A besom is a broom made of twigs tied around a stick.

You can also cleanse the area by passing your hands in counter-clockwise circles as you walk in ever-larger counter-clockwise circles around the intended ritual area if the flooring is delicate.

Ringing a bell or striking a singing bowl, again while walking in counter-clockwise circles, will also cleanse the area.

Mark the center of your planned circle. A centrally positioned altar is good if you are carrying out a mainly altar-centered ceremony, as you then receive directly the concentrated power of the central axis. Alternatively, you can place the altar about a third of the way within the circle toward the north of the planned circle area.

WHAT SIZE SHOULD A CIRCLE BE?

A circle, always cast clockwise, should enclose yourself and anyone working with you, your altar, and your tools if you are using them.

Traditionally circles are nine feet in diameter, but the exact measurement isn't required. If there are many people in the circle, or if you and others want to dance, move around, or face the four directions in turn to greet the Guardians, then it is better to create a circle with a larger diameter. Go with what feels right. It is better to have a larger circle than to be short of room. In time, you won't worry about measurements but will know instinctively what feels right. You can create a really large circle if you are inviting lots of people to a collective ceremony, perhaps to celebrate a seasonal change point.

For guidance, set four flat stones in advance around the envisaged circumference at the main directions. You could also place directional candles in advance (all white or beeswax, or torches).

CIRCLE-CASTING IN RITUALS

In the Northern magickal tradition, circles are generally cast north to north, but if you prefer, you can start with the east.

Whatever form of circle is cast, even if you are not personally creating it (like at a public ritual), visualize the circle of light spreading as it's cast. This will strengthen it as well as create a personal connection.

If you are casting the circle, whether actual or visualized, to tap into the power, first raise light throughout your whole body from the root chakra energy center to the crown.

Picture light pouring in from all around: red upward from the earth for the root or base; silver or orange from the moon for the navel sacral; yellow from the sun, the central top of the stomach for the solar plexus; green from nature for the heart; sky blue from the angels for the throat; indigo or purple from the archangels and Elemental Guardians for the brow chakra; and white, gold, or violet from the deities for the crown energy center.

Visualize the rainbow colors merging into pure-white light within you and radiating from you.

Wiggle your fingers, and you will sense if not see them glowing.

Then, also before circle-casting, you would make your opening blessing, standing in the center and turning slowly to face all directions as you speak. This is sometimes referred to as the call to ritual and might alternatively be blowing a horn, using a singing bowl, or using bells to make sound. Other people begin with a poetic piece from their own or a traditional Book of Shadows, a special book in which you record your magickal rituals and associations.

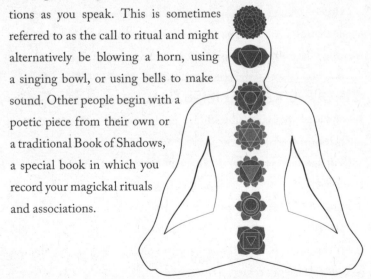

MAKING A PHYSICAL CIRCLE

Before a spell or ritual, you can create a permanent circle made of stones, shells, or crystals, or construct one from herbs, flowers, or branches as a communal activity. This circle is to be empowered before commencing the spell or ritual. The stones from which you build your circle don't have to connect but give an outline.

You can also paint a circle on the floor in a room you regularly use for magick and cover it with a large rug, find a special large circular carpet, or chalk one outdoors on pavement.

Alternatively, use tea lights indoors or outdoors to make a circle. Light these clockwise in a circle shape at the start of the ceremony before empowering the circle, or make the lighting the casting activity. If you have several people, or a coven, the tea lights can be lit by participants. Each person lights their own tea lights and speaks a blessing or wish in turn, clockwise, one after the other, after making the body of light and the opening blessing.

Use a natural existing outdoor circle, such as a grove of trees. Always ask permission from the natural essences of the place.

Draw a circle clockwise in the earth, snow, or sand with a long stick or a sword. Try to do it in a single sweep.

Best of all is the circle of people linking hands one by one, starting in the north. While this is happening, the person carrying out the ritual stands in the center, turning slowly. Each participant can make a spoken blessing, one after the other, saying, for example: *The circle of love knows no limits.*

SYMBOLIC CIRCLE-CASTING

Even with a physical circle, unless you use the joining hands or tea-light method of casting, you will need to empower and so activate the circle in one of the ways described in this section. However, a Wiccan circle can be cast purely symbolically or clairvoyantly, which involves walking around the visualized circle area clockwise with a sword, wand, pointed quartz crystal, or athame to create a psychic circle of light.

Form this psychic light circle in the air, about waist or knee high, whichever feels more natural.

Hold your crystal, wand, athame, or sword in your power hand, the one you write with. Direct the point at about a 45-degree angle, casting the circle in front of you so you step into the emerging light and become empowered.

Enclose the circle by stepping inside the completed circle yourself and turning your body to close the circle afterward (at the north).

Make a circle-casting chant that you repeat either aloud or in your mind as you walk. For example: *May the circle be cast and remain unbroken. May the love of the Goddess be forever in my/our heart(s). Blessings be on this rite and all present.*

All includes the deities, nature essences, wise ancestors, etc.

You may wish to create a dome of light over the top of the circle with the wand or athame. From the center of the circle, turn on the spot, moving the athame in an arch upward and outward in clockwise spirals, or leave your temple open to the sun, moon, and stars.

MAKING A TRIPLE ELEMENTAL CIRCLE

Another method is to use salt water, incense, and the flame of a candle to cast your circle.

Light the candle and incense in advance at the altar and then carry them outside the visualized circle, placing them on a rock or small table.

Consecrate the salt water for the circle at the altar (as you did when you were dedicating the tools and altar after the opening call), and again, take it outside the circle. For additional power, some practitioners use the triple elemental casting after drawing the circle of light around a symbolic circle.

If the circle is an existing physical one, you can empower it psychically by walking around the outline three times *deosil* (clockwise), once with each of the three elemental substances: sacred salt water, incense, and candle flame, or salt, incense, and water. With a group, three people can walk clockwise around the circle in procession, one after the other, carrying the three substances in that order.

Make the circles one on top of the other, and end the triple elemental casting by sprinkling each person present with a few drops of the sacred salt water. After you have entered the circle, again walk clockwise around its inside, saying: *You are blessed and welcome.*

If you are working alone, end the triple circle–casting by taking the salt water and sprinkling yourself, saying: *May the Lord and Lady, Goddess and God, bless my spell/ritual.*

VISUALIZING THE CIRCLE OF LIGHT

You can do this when you want a quick spell or if you are in a place where you can't physically walk around a circle area.

If there is little privacy, visualize the circle appearing around you as though drawn with a glowing wand of golden light while standing or siting still, facing north.

However, if you do have some privacy, stand in the center of your area facing where you think north is. Holding a pointed quartz crystal, your wand when practical (I have a very tiny crystal one), or subtly extending the index finger of your power hand at waist height, turn your body and feet slowly in a circle, but remain in the same spot. Picture light flowing outward, creating a circle around you. Make the circle of visualized gold, white, silver, or blue light in one sweeping (and, if necessary, subtle) continuous movement of your hand.

UNCASTING THE CIRCLE

Some people do not uncast a circle but consider closing the four elemental Watchtowers at the four directions and blowing out any directional/elemental candles before making a closing blessing sufficient (see page 36). This is especially so with a natural circle of trees or a circle made of stones or shells, in which case you would remove the final piece that was set down in order to allow the energies to flow freely. The energies will soon dissipate, and you can replace the stones after twenty-four hours.

However, uncasting the circle after a ceremony is a way of restoring the ritual place and participants to their earlier state even though they're now blessed, which, in the case of an altar room, will make it harmonious and peaceful rather than buzzing.

Uncasting circles counter-clockwise, or moonwise—or *widdershins*, the Wiccan term for *counter-clockwise*—completes what was set up clockwise, or *deosil*/sunwise.

To uncast any circle, however cast, after the ceremonies and all present have been thanked and asked to return to their own place, walk around counter-clockwise from north back to north in the Northern magickal tradition (or east to east as others prefer) with the wand/athame, etc., behind you. All the while, picture the light returning to the source, finger, crystal, or wand. As you do so, say a closing chant, such as: *May the circle be open yet remain unbroken in our hearts and in our lives. Blessed be.* or *Blessings be on all.*

Alternatively stand in the center facing north and turn counter-clockwise in one spot, drawing the light back into its source, or picture the radiance sinking into the ground as you turn.

In the next chapter, we will explore the world of the elements and the elemental Guardians who bring their energies to any magick.

WICCA AND
THE MAGICKAL
ELEMENTS

THE FOUR MAGICKAL ELEMENTS THAT CORRESPOND WITH the four main directions of the altar and the magick circle offer a treasury of symbolism to enrich rituals: Earth for enhancing practical needs such as sufficient money, the right home, and stability; Air for swift results and where matters of the mind such as examinations or communication in interviews are involved, Fire for inspiration and power; and Water for love and relationships or family matters.

The fusing of these elements creates, it is believed by magickal practitioners, spiritual energy called Aether, Akasha, or Spirit, in which thoughts and desires can be animated and transferred (or rather catapulted) into material reality.

THE ELEMENTS IN MAGICK

The following associations are the most usual, rooted in traditional magick, but if you study other forms of Wicca, you may find variations that suit you better; for example, variations of color.

Earth

Time of Day: Midnight

Time of Life: Old age, and so wisdom and tradition

Season: Winter

Elemental Tool: Pentacle

Sacred Elemental Substance: Salt

Elemental Creature: Gnome

Colors: Green or golden brown

Tarot Suit: Pentacles, discs, or coins

Guardian of North Wind: Boreas

Energy Raising: Drumming

Deities: All Earth Mothers, Creatrix goddesses, Mistress of Animals, and Crone/Wise Woman goddesses, also Earth Fathers, Horned God, and gods of the hunt (see Chapters 6 and 7 on Gods and Goddesses)

Archangel: Uriel, archangel of protection, transformation, and guardian of the earth and sun who brought alchemy to humankind, described as having an open hand holding a flame, dressing in rich burnished gold and ruby red with a bright flamelike halo blazing in the darkness, and wielding a fiery sword that flashes lightning

Crystals: Most agates, especially moss and tree (dendritic) agate, amazonite, aventurine, emerald, fossils, jet, malachite, petrified or fossilized wood, rose quartz, rutilated quartz, smoky quartz, red and gold tigereye, and all stones with holes in the center

Power Animals and Birds: Antelope, badger, bear, boar, cow, bull, dog, stag, sheep, squirrel, rabbit, snake, bee, spider, and wolf

Point on Pentagram: Lower left

Physical and Psychic Senses: Touch and taste, also psychometry and clairsentience

Fragrances: Cypress, fern, geranium, heather, hibiscus, honeysuckle, magnolia, oakmoss, patchouli, sagebrush, sweetgrass, vervain, and vetivert

Positive Qualities: Patience, stability, generosity, reliability, endurance, perseverance, respect for others and traditions, protectiveness, fertility (also contained in Water), acceptance of others as they are and of self, grounding, tolerance, and caretaker of the environment

Earth Places: Caves, crypts, ley lines, forests, ice, snow, rocks, mountains (also a place of Air), gardens, temples, old stone circles, and homes

Materials (Substances and Phenomena): Salt, herbs, flowers, trees, coins, bread, corn and wheat, fabrics, nuts, clay, grass, soil, sand, berries, potpourri, herbs, crystals and gems, and plants

Natural Associations: Earth lights, crop circles, fields of grain, sand storms, earthquakes and tremors, land guardians or Landvættir, and the ancestors

Astrological Signs: Capricorn, Virgo, and Taurus

Planets: Venus and Saturn

Keywords: "I accept and nurture all."

Use Earth in Magick for: Protection; property; the home and all domestic matters; for stability in any area of your life; for a steady infusion of money and banishing debt; official matters; for families and animals; for crystal, herb, and all environmental magick; and for spells concerning institutions such as the law, politics, finance, health, and education. It is also a focus for all rituals against famine, deforestation, land pollution, devastation through unwise building or industrialization, and for caring for animals and their natural habitats.

Air

Time of Day: Dawn

Time of Life: Birth/rebirth and childhood

Season: Spring

Elemental Tool: Sword

Sacred Elemental Substance: Incense or smudge

Elemental Creature: Sylph

Colors: Yellow or gray

Tarot suit: Swords

Guardian of the East Wind: Eolus

Energy Raising: Music and song

Deities: Maiden, spring, and flower goddesses; deities of light, Sky Fathers and Mothers, gods, and goddesses; messenger and healing deities; and star deities (also sometimes seen as fire)

Archangel: Raphael, archangel of healing, the four winds and the traveler's archangel, described as carrying a golden vial of medicine and a traveler's staff, dressed in the colors of early morning sunlight, a green healing ray emanating from his halo

Crystals: Amethyst, angelite, blue lace agate, clear crystal quartz (also fire), citrine, diamond, Herkimer diamond, danburite, lapis lazuli, sodalite, sugilite, sapphire, and turquoise

Power Animals and Birds: Eagle, hawk, nightingale, birds of prey, white dove, winged insects, and butterfly

Point of the Pentagram: Upper left

Physical and Psychic Senses: Hearing; also, clairaudience

Fragrances: Acacia, almond, anise, benzoin, bergamot, dill, fennel, lavender, lemongrass, lemon verbena, lily of the valley, marjoram, meadowsweet, papyrus flower, peppermint, and sage

Positive Qualities: Communication skills, persuasiveness, joy, focus, intelligence, fair mindedness, logic, independence, clarity, good memory, mental dexterity, optimism, teaching abilities, poetic and musical gifts, concentration, commercial and technological acumen, versatility, and healing gifts through orthodox medicine or from higher sources

Air Places: Mountaintops, hills, towers, steeples and spires, the sky, pyramids, open plains, tall buildings, balconies, roof gardens, and the sky

Materials (Substances and Phenomena): Fragrance oils, flowers, wind chimes, feathers, four winds, clouds, balloons, kites, feathers, air-borne seeds and spores, smoke, winds, whirlwinds, hurricanes, storms, boats with sails billowing in the wind, and weathervanes

Natural Associations: Clouds, light, the life force, spirits, ghosts (believed to enfold themselves in the wind to travel), angels, elves, and fairies

Astrological Associations: Aquarius, Libra, and Gemini

Planets: Mercury, Jupiter, and Uranus

Use Air in Magick for: Passing tests and examinations; for learning; for travel; for changes and improvements in career; for house moves; for money-raising ventures, as well as anything to do with science, technology, or the media; for healing the ozone layer and slowing down global warming; to recover lost or stolen items; to uncover the truth; for new beginnings; and for feather magick

Fire

Time of Day: Noon

Time of Life: Young adulthood, finding a partner, and producing offspring

Season: Summer

Elemental Tool: Wand

Sacred Elemental Substance: Candle

Elemental Creature: Salamander, the magickal lizard creature believed to live in fire

Colors: Red, orange, or gold

Tarot Suit: Wands, rods, or staves

Guardian of the South Wind: Notus

Energy Raising: Dance and ritual fires

Deities: All fire gods and goddesses, deities of passion and seduction, blacksmith and metal-working deities, and deities of the sun

Archangel: Michael, archangel of the sun, supreme archangel, who oversees the natural world, including the weather; leader of all the great warrior angels and traditional dragon slayers; described as having golden wings and red and gold armor with a sword, a shield, a green date branch, and carrying the scales of justice or a white banner with a red cross

Crystals: Amber, bloodstone, Boji stones, carnelian, garnet, lava, iron pyrites, obsidian, ruby, and topaz

Animals and Birds: Cat, lion, cougar, stag, dragon, firefly, dragonfly, and the legendary golden phoenix (symbol of transformation and rebirth, which burns itself on a funeral pyre every five-hundred years, only to rise again golden from the ashes)

Point on pentagram: Lower right

Physical and Psychic Senses: Vision and clairvoyance

Fragrances: Allspice, angelica, basil, bay, carnation, cedarwood, chamomile, cinnamon, cloves, copal, dragon's blood, frankincense, heliotrope, juniper, lime, marigold, nutmeg, orange, rosemary, and tangerine

Positive Qualities: Courage, inspiration, idealism and altruism, fidelity, striving for perfection, defense of the weak, intuition, imagination, creativity, leadership, good health, transformation, fertility in all aspects of life (also ruled by Earth and Water), transformation, courage, mysticism, clairvoyance, prophecy, determination to overcome any obstacle, energy, living spirit, and abundance

Fire Places: The family hearth, deserts, shimmering sand, hilltop beacons, red rock formations, and altars with candles

Substances (Materials and Phenomena): Candles, beeswax, flames, ash, fiber-optic lamps, lightning, jack-o'-lanterns, clear crystal spheres, gold, mirrors, oranges, suncatchers, sunflowers, and all golden flowers; also, volcanoes, forest fires, and solar eclipses

Natural Associations: Blood, the sun, ritual and hearth fires, stars (sometimes also associated with Air), bonfires, comets, rainbows, meteors, lightning, torches (wood was believed to contain fire that could be released by friction), djinns (genies), and fire fairies

Astrological signs: Aries, Leo, and Sagittarius

Planets: Sun and Mars

Use Fire in Magick for: Fulfilling ambitions; for wise power and leadership; all creative and artistic ventures; religion and spirituality; success in sports and competitive games; for courage; to increase psychic powers (especially higher ones such as channeling); for pleasure, passion, and the consummation of love; for sacred sex; the removal of what is no longer needed; binding and banishing; protection against a vicious attack or threats; for candle magick; for protection against drought; to combat all pollution caused by burning fuels or chemicals, as well as forest fires and the slash-and-burn policy that threatens rainforests.

Water

Time of Day: Sunset or twilight

Time of Life: Middle years right through retirement and the Third Age

Season: Fall/Autumn

Elemental Tool: Chalice

Sacred Elemental Substance: Water

Elemental Creature: Nymph

Colors: Blue or silver

Tarot Suit: Cups or Chalices

Guardian of the West Wind: Zephyrus

Energy Raising: Rattles, prayer, and chanting

Deities: Moon and love deities; sea, sacred well, and water gods and goddesses; and goddesses of initiation and the mystery religions

Archangel: Gabriel, archangel of the moon, divine messenger carrying divine messages, regarded as having female energies. She is described as being clothed in silver or dark blue with a mantle of stars and a crescent moon for her halo, a golden horn, and a white lily, or alternatively with a lantern in her right hand and a mirror made of jasper in her left

Crystals: Aquamarine, calcite, coral, jade, moonstone, fluorite, pearl, opal, and tourmaline

Animals and Birds: Frog; dolphin; otter and beaver; heron; duck; seal; whale; swan and all water birds; all fish, especially the salmon; starfish; crab; sea horse; and crocodile and alligator

Point on Pentagram: Upper right

Physical and Psychic Senses: Sixth sense/intuition; also, healing, telepathy, and scrying

Fragrances: Apple blossom, apricot, coconut, eucalyptus, feverfew, heather, hyacinth, jasmine, lemon, lemon balm, lilac, lily, myrrh, orchid, passionflower, peach, strawberry, sweet pea, thyme, valerian, vanilla, and violet

Positive Qualities: Beauty, compassion, empathy, peacemaking, harmony, sympathy, love, forgiveness, unconscious wisdom, purity, ability to merge and interconnect with nature, the cycles of the seasons, and the life cycle

Water Places: Pools, streams, estuaries, waterfalls, sacred wells and springs, whirlpools, rivers, the sea, marshland, flood plains, aquariums, and water parks

Natural Associations: The moon, rain, ritual baths, mists, fog, dreams, mermaids, and water sprites

Materials (Substances and Phenomena): Milk, wine, sea shells, crystal spheres, scrying bowls, dark mirrors, reflections in water, tides, floods, and tsunamis

Astrological Associations: Pisces, Cancer, and Scorpio

Planets: Neptune, the moon, and Pluto

Use Water in Magick for: Love, relationships, friendships, the mending of quarrels, astral travel, protection of those far away, dreams, purification rites, healing, using the powers of nature and especially water (particularly sacred water), scrying, divination, all water and sea magick, moon magick, and travel by sea. It is also potent for fighting floods; cleansing sea, lake, and river pollution; in campaigns for fresh water to parts of the world where there is none; world health initiatives; and care of whales, dolphins, seals, and all endangered sea creatures.

USING THE ELEMENTS RATHER THAN DIRECTIONS AS A GUIDE TO CIRCLE-CASTING

Some practitioners in the southern hemisphere use the northern hemisphere traditional clockwise circle-casting and north-facing altar positions, recognizing that Wicca was originally a northern hemisphere tradition.

However, other southern practitioners cast the circle in their sunwise or *deosil* direction, which in the southern world is counter-clockwise, and uncast moonwise or *widdershins*, which is clockwise to them.

More problematic in the southern hemisphere are the directions, since they are opposite from the north. For example, the cold regions traditionally associated with Earth in the northern hemisphere in Wicca are south toward the Antarctic for the southern hemisphere. In the same way, heat is north toward the equator, and the seaboard for Water may be on the east for the southern hemisphere.

The best way around this is to work purely with the elements, not the directions, and disassociate from the north. For example with Earth, make the altar and circle position for Earth as the direction toward the most solid land mass wherever you are casting magick. Fire would be the direction of heat, Water the nearest ocean or water source, and Air the mountains or plains.

WELCOMING THE ELEMENTAL GUARDIANS INTO YOUR CAST CIRCLE

After circle-casting, many Wiccans in ritual call upon the Guardians of each elemental quadrant of the circle, often called the Guardians of the Watchtowers, and generally begin with Earth.

In the northern hemisphere, the Guardians are welcomed clockwise around the circle. Earth followed by Air, followed by Fire, followed by Water and counter-clockwise in the southern hemisphere, again starting with Earth.

The Elemental Guardians add their various powers to energize and give life and form to the elements such as salt, incense, candle flame, and water on the altar. The Guardians may be identified as deities (north and west are traditionally represented by female deity energy forms, though this can vary per the culture; archangels; power animals; or elemental spirits). You can refer to the association lists in this chapter or to the deities section in Chapter 3 (page 22).

In formal magick the Guardians are often called the Lords and/or Ladies of the Watchtowers.

These wise protectors are very important and guard the circle from all earthly negative feelings and any external pressures from the outside world. Because you are working with spiritual powers, the Guardians will also prevent anything less than benign from entering the sacred space while you are spiritually open and vulnerable during ritual.

DISCOVERING YOUR PERSONAL ELEMENTAL GUARDIANS

If you are working alone, sit in each quadrant of your circle in turn and allow a figure of a person, animal, bird, or sea creature to come into your mind quite naturally as representing the Guardian of that elemental quadrant. If you are meditating together as part of a coven exercise before ritual, you could divide coven members into groups and allow each group to work with visualization to evoke a collective vision of their chosen element.

When you see in your mind's vision an Elemental Guardian for each of the four Quarters, allow a name to come for each of them. It may be a name you can identify afterward online or in a book, or your elemental spirit or angel may adopt this appearance and name exclusively for you.

Next, decide how you will ask each Guardian to enter your circle after the circle-casting, and at the end of your ritual before uncasting the circle, decide how you will thank them and bid them farewell.

OPENING THE ELEMENTAL QUARTERS IN RITUAL

A chosen person—either you or another member of the coven chosen to represent each quadrant—faces outward to the chosen element center point, beginning with Earth, and draws the invoking or attracting pentagram in front of themselves in the air, knee to shoulder high, and anyone else present can do the same. Then, raising both arms high with palms flat and uppermost and then lowering them, you can make a greeting to each Guardian in turn with such words as, *Guardian of the Watchtower of Earth, you are welcome and I/we ask your protection and blessings on this ritual.*

As you welcome the Elemental Guardians and the gateways open, you may see or sense the worlds they inhabit. For instance, through the Earth doorway you may sense or glimpse rich green forests or ripening corn, and through the Fire doorway you may see the brilliant sun.

After the ritual, before uncasting, it is necessary to close the Quarters. You or the person designated to the element would draw the banishing pentagram again in front of you in the air and others can do the same (some begin the closing with the Water element), and go around the circle counter-clockwise in the northern hemisphere and clockwise in the southern hemisphere until all four Quarters are closed.

At each Quarter, before drawing the closing pentagram, you should raise your arms as before and then lower them, thanking the Guardians in turn, and say: *Hail and farewell. Until we meet again.*

It is always important, especially with elemental spirits, to close the doors of the Watchtowers, as otherwise magickal forces can remain in the cosmos and become thought forms or tulpas (a *tulpa* is a being or object that is created through sheer spiritual or mental discipline alone), and with elemental energies this is not advisable. So alternatively, say: *Wise Guardian of [element], I offer you blessings until we meet again.*

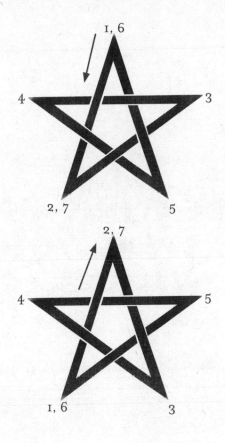

In the next chapter, we will look at magickal timings and further magickal associations such as colors, fragrances, and crystals you can add to enhance spells and rituals.

CREATING AND CASTING YOUR OWN SPELLS

A S A WICCAN, MUCH OF YOUR WORK WILL INVOLVE CASTING spells on behalf of others, for those who request them; spells you carry out for yourself, your family, friends, animals, or anyone in need; as well as spells to send healing to places and people who are suffering.

SPELLS, RITUALS, AND WICCAN CEREMONIES

The words *spells* and *rituals* are often interchangeable. A spell tends to be less formal and structured than a ritual, and is usually cast for a specific purpose, person, place, or need, and requires results within a specific time frame. In contrast, a ritual may not just be a means to achieve a desired result, but a purpose in itself such as calling down the power of the moon on a night of a full moon to channel the wisdom of the Goddess (covens hold their monthly *esbats*, or gatherings, on the night of the full moon) or for a wider intention such as furthering world peace.

Ceremonies that we will cover in Chapter 8 tend to be even more elaborate rituals to which non-Wiccans or family members are often invited—for example, a Handfasting (Wiccan wedding), a Baby-Naming, or a celebration on the Autumn Equinox to give thanks for abundance received during the year and to ask for sufficient supply for the months ahead.

In rituals and ceremonies, there tends to be a more elaborate structure, including a blessing of the salt and water and the opening of the four Quarters.

YOUR BOOK OF SHADOWS

Once you begin spell-casting, you may wish to record the spells you create in a private Book of Shadows. This is every practitioner's personal source book, inspiration, magickal diary, and a legacy for future generations. It contains recorded information about herbs and incenses, crystals, and different moon phases and their energies, and if you belong to a coven there will be a collective Book of Shadows for recording coven magickal workings.

A Book of Shadows is, even in these technological times, always handwritten. You can buy leather or fabric blank page books and should write with a nib pen and ink if possible (green on cream paper or black on white). Best of all but not essential are the kind with a binder where blank pages can be inserted. This will allow you to add and revise material.

As a modern witch, an online copy of the most relevant parts of the written Book of Shadows is valuable, especially for exchanging information with other witches and because physical books can be lost or destroyed.

In addition, have a notebook small enough to carry with you whenever you have a day out, a weekend, or a holiday for recording information about any new plants or herbs you see growing, legends of wells, ancient sites, museum visits, local rhymes and chants, and churches and cathedrals.

THE SIX STAGES OF SPELL-CASTING

There are six stages in casting a spell. It is important to observe them all, although you can vary slightly from these guidelines if you feel it is appropriate in your practice.

Stage 1: Defining the Purpose of the Spell

I have described northern hemisphere positions, but you can adapt these in the southern hemisphere as suggested in the previous chapter. As you formulate your spell, consider your ideal timeframe for results to manifest in the everyday world, unless you prefer to say *when the time is right for fulfillment*.

Is the spell a one-time only or does it need to be repeated daily for a week, monthly, or when the particular situation addressed in the spell arises? If ongoing, will you need to cast it again when the fragrance of a spell bag fades?

Next, you'll need to find or create a symbol into which you will put the magickal spell power, for example:

- Representative items to be sent after the spell, such as a plant to someone who is ill or coins for prosperity.

- A bag of herbs chosen for their magickal meanings in a small drawstring bag of the appropriate color, or a crystal—each of which has magickal significance.

- A written message to be burned in the candle flame.

- Colored candles (see Chapter 10, page 100, for color significance), with three or four words that represent the spell purpose etched on the side of each unlit candle. The vowels are often omitted in written messages and the words joined.

- Small fabric dolls or featureless play-clay, dough, or beeswax figures to represent lovers, family, or a sick person. Craft an image on a slightly melted beeswax sheet: a heart for love, a plane for long-distance travel, or a baby in a cradle for fertility, to name a few.

- Tarot cards, such as the King and Queen of Cups, the Lovers for love and marriage, the World for travel, and the Wheel of Fortune for attracting good luck.

- A cord, strong thread, or ribbon for tying a knot that afterward can be released for power or luck, left bound to restrain bad behavior or destructive people, burned in a candle flame to banish a destructive relationship or fears, or hung from a tree for slow release by decay or weather.

- Stones or bones marked with appropriate images that can be buried or cast into water.

Stage 2: Setting the Scene

- Set the symbol on a dish in the center of the altar or spell table, plus the four elemental substances: salt, incense, candle, and water.

- Visualize a circle of light enclosing you, the altar, and anyone present clockwise.

- If working alone start with *I am* followed by your secret magickal name and ask your guardian angels, a favorite archangel, the Goddess, or the power of light and goodness to protect you and help your magickal endeavor.

- Light candles being used and, from them, an incense stick, then state aloud the purpose of the spell while holding the symbol, or, if in a group, passing it around so each person can verbally define the purpose.

Stage 3: Setting the Energies in Motion

- To endow the symbol and spoken intention of the spell with elemental power, pass the symbol around, over, or through the four elemental substances in turn. Alternatively, keep the symbol in the center of the altar and sprinkle/pass the elements around it.

- Begin with the salt in the north, then the incense in the east, the candle in the south, and the water in the west, and for each element add empowering words, such as *I call success/love/healing with the power of Earth/Air/Fire/Water.*

Stage 4: Raising or Increasing the Elemental Power

This is the most active and powerful part of the spell, and it involves building up the speed and intensity of the elemental action to combine the elements to create the fifth element Aether, Akasha, or Spirit, the magickal space and energy where transformation from intention to actuality takes place.

- Dance, drum, chant, or do all of these at the same time as you circle the altar.

- Tie knots in a cord and then toss it rhythmically in your cupped hands.

- Mix your herbs together in a bowl with a spoon or mortar and pestle faster and faster and then add them to the bag, closing it and tossing it in the air.

- Toss the symbol, if a crystal or small solid item, progressively higher in the air.

- If in a group, pass the symbol faster and faster around the circle, with a chant spoken faster and faster, such as *Power of the magick, power of the spell, power of the magick, use the magick well.*

- If working alone, enchant the symbol with the palms of both hands by holding your hands palms down and flat a few centimeters above the symbol in the center of the altar.

- If outdoors, spiral a smudge stick in huge circles, allowing it to dictate its own pathway and shapes.

- If indoors, swirl a pair of lighted incense sticks, one held in each hand, a few centimeters above the symbol, while the right incense stick or hand moves clockwise and the left one counter-clockwise.

- Regardless of method, move your hands, self, etc. faster and faster and create a chant to draw in all four elemental powers, likewise sung or spoken faster and faster, with ever more volume and speed until the words are no longer separate.

- A popular Wiccan repetitive chant is *Earth, Air, Water, Fire, bring to me what I desire.*

- A slightly more complex chant to raise the power is *Water, Air, Fire, and Earth, bring I ask this wish to birth*, followed by *Water* [pause], *Air,* [pause], *Fire* [pause], *Earth,* [pause].

- As the power, speed, and intensity grow, whether alone or in a coven, circle the altar, changing the chant to *The power of the Earth* [clap and stomp], *the power of the Air* [clap and stomp], *the power of the Fire* [clap and stomp], *the power of the Water* [clap and stomp].

- Other spell chants include Goddess names, the most popular sung all over the world being Isis, Astarte [or Diana, Hecate, Demeter, or Kali], or Inanna (see Chapter 6 [page 65] to learn more of these Goddesses).

- Move, drum, stomp, clap, or chant until you feel that the power has reached its height. This is like revving a car with the hand brake on or piloting a plane whose wheels are starting to lift off the tarmac.

An Alternative Stage 4

- If you are casting a healing spell or letting go of sorrow or pain, rather than releasing the power into the cosmos, gently push the power into, for example, a healing herb bag mix or a soft-colored crystal you have used as the spell focus.

- Build up the power until you have almost reached the crescendo. Hold the raised energy for a moment, keeping your voice and your movements steady, and then begin to recite the words more softly and make any actions slower.

- Keep reducing your movements and words until your words fade from a whisper to silence as your actions cease.

- Point down with incense sticks or the closed fingers of both hands toward the symbol at a 45-degree angle (slightly away if necessary so no ash falls on the symbol, herbs, or crystals), so the power and light flow directly into the symbol. Say *May the light or power of the Goddess/archangel [name] enter here and so bring peace/healing. Blessings be on all.*

Creating and Casting Your Own Spells

- When you feel the power has passed into the symbol, stand motionless or silent for a moment, return the incense sticks to their holders to burn away, and put your hands in front of you facing down so any residual power can flow into the earth.

Stage 5: Ways of Releasing the Power

When you or the person leading the spell feels the moment is right, you will release the power into the cosmos. The more you cast spells the more easily you will become aware, toward the end of Stage 4, of a spiraling rainbow vortex (often called a cone of power) above you. This now will explode around you in a glorious firework display. Some people see this clairvoyantly in their inner vision or sense it.

To Release the Spell Power Into the Cosmos

Raise incense sticks and hold them upright above your head, calling *The power is free, the power's in me.* Plunge the incense sticks simultaneously into a bowl of sand, soil, or water to extinguish them. Lift your hands and upstretched arms high on either side of your head, then swing them behind you and forward waist high in a slashing movement, then down again.

Make a final shout, clap, stomp, leap, or drum roll as you call out *The power is free. The wish is mine* or *I am pure Spirit.*

Stage 6: Moving to a Conclusion

- Without making a sound, hold the symbol and allow the energies to synthesize and flow. If you are working as a group, pass the symbol around slowly for each person to endow it

A LITTLE BIT OF WICCA

with silent or quietly spoken blessings. Any energies that were released into the cosmos will fill the symbol and your aura energy field and that of anyone present.

- Extinguish any remaining candles and make a spoken farewell blessing and thanks to the Guardians who protected you.

- Visualize the circle light fading in the reverse direction from which you called it.

- If the symbol is for someone who is not present, send it to the absent person or, if not practical, keep it next to a photo of them.

- Finally, sit on the ground and press down with your hands and feet on the earth to let excess unfocused energy drain out. Alternatively, stand with your feet apart and your hands by your sides, fingers pointing downward, and feel yourself gradually slowing down and your body and mind relaxing. You should also do this after rituals.

- Tidy up the area, and as you are ready to leave the spell place, whisper softly or say in your mind: *The rite is finished. Blessings be on all.*

In the next chapter, we will learn how to create Wiccan rituals.

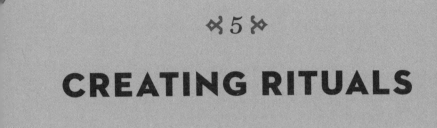

❖ 5 ❖

CREATING RITUALS

WHILE SOME WICCANS QUITE HAPPILY AND VERY SUC-
cessfully focus on spell-casting, rituals are the next,
more formal, stage of magick. Like spells, rituals can
be carried out alone or with others. You may recognize some of the
stages I describe in this chapter from earlier chapters, but now we
will now learn about them in more detail.

In Chapter 6, for example, I describe the ritual of Drawing
Down the Moon, variations of which many solitary practitioners,
informal magick groups, and more formal covens practice monthly
on the full moon. After reading this chapter, you will have the tools
to perform it yourself. There is no limit to what you can perform
rituals for. You can send peace or healing to areas suffering through
war, drought, or other natural disasters, or even to disadvantaged
people who are struggling with poverty or disease. You can offer
strength to anyone who needs it. However, rituals can simply give

thanks for blessings received, ask for a private or collective blessing, or ask for help.

Many rituals are centered around rites of passage such as Handfasting; the passing of a beloved friend, family, or coven member, or a figure who has done good in the world; a Baby-Naming ceremony; or at seasonal change points to give strength to the year. These will be discussed in detail later in the book.

OFFERINGS IN RITUAL

Offerings, which are usually natural materials such as flowers/petals, herbs, or crystals, often take the place of a focused symbol, and as you make them you can request enough for your needs and a little more, and in return offer your service to others and the planet. Each of these has a magickal significance that you can discover in Chapter 10 (page 95). Note that for ease I am using northern hemisphere directions and associations in all these descriptions.

Pre-Ritual

Decide the right time and date for the ritual as well as appropriate incense fragrances, candle colors, etc., again using the references in Chapter 10.

If working ritually with a coven or less formal magickal group, decide in advance the format you will follow and who will be responsible for particular parts of the ritual. If working alone, draw up a written plan but carry out the ritual without notes as spontaneity and an open heart are what matter. Only in very formal magick is total precision necessary.

Prepare yourself by bathing or anointing your four main energy center points and putting on a loose robe you keep for the occasion (see Chapter 1, page 1, for information on dedicating the altar) either before or immediately after asperging the area of the planned circle.

STAGE 1: PREPARING THE RITUAL AREA

Cleanse the anticipated circle area by asperging or sprinkling it with a small bundle of twigs dipped in water and/or sweeping (see Chapter 2, page 13, for information on circle-casting).

Indoors, smudge the room with an herbal smoke stick in cedar or sagebrush, or a cedar or pine incense stick, in alternate clockwise and counter-clockwise circles. Both indoors and out, add a chant as you work, such as: *May only goodness and light remain here and may this area be dedicated for the greatest good and highest purpose.*

Set up your altar with the four magickal substances, a bowl of salt, incense, candle, and water bowl, and as many or as few of the magickal tools listed on page 3 as you choose. Include the pentacle in the north, the athame or knife in the east, the wand in the south, and the chalice in the west, each to the right of its own elemental substance. You may wish to refer back to Chapter 1, page 2, for information on setting the altar.

In the center of the altar, set an offerings bowl for your symbolic offerings (use a mini cauldron if you wish). A normal-size cauldron is good for use outdoors at a larger gathering; it can serve as the central offerings repository.

Before beginning the ritual, pass your hands over the altar nine times—the one you write with clockwise and the other counter-clockwise, palms down. Say nine times: *Blessings be on this altar and this ritual. May my/our magick be only for the greatest good and with the purest intention.* I have noticed that even in the southern hemisphere, for raising power, most practitioners use the northern clockwise/power hand and counter-clockwise/receptive hand.

Light charcoal beforehand if you are using granular incense as opposed to sticks or cones.

STAGE 2: MARK THE BEGINNING OF THE RITUAL FORMALLY

Ring the bell at each of the Quarters of the circle, whether physical or visualized. If you are using a pre-constructed one, start in the north where the bell is. Then make an opening blessing and ask for the protection of God and Goddess, the power of light, or specific deities, facing north, or if others are present, standing in the center of the visualized circle, slowly turning in all directions as you speak.

Raise your arms high and wide as you say something like *Bless this ritual, Mother and Father, keep harm beyond and peace within. Bless me/all who gather here/this day* or *By earth and sky and sea be blessed, by moon and sun and stars be sanctified.*

Light the Goddess candle and, from it, the God candle, left to right.

Bless the salt and water and add salt to the water bowl, as you did in Chapter 1 when dedicating your tools. Make the cross first in the salt, then the water bowl with the athame.

Light the elemental south candle, and if you are using four directional altar candles light those north to west clockwise, which would make two candles in total in the south.

Light any incense cones or incense sticks from the Goddess candle, or sprinkle some incense mix on the charcoal, which should be white hot.

STAGE 3: CASTING THE CIRCLE

You may wish to refer back to Chapter 2, page 13.

In a group rite, after the blessing and before circle-casting, you can lead all those present into the ritual area, all joining hands and spiraling until you make a physical circle joined by hands, left palm up, right palm down. Then create the magickal circle around them and signal the dropping of hands.

Walk around the inside of the circle, and, as they face you, sprinkle each one with a few drops of water or salt water, saying *Blessed be* or *You are welcome.*

Sprinkle yourself with the sacred salt water if working alone, returning to the altar after circle-casting, facing north.

STAGE 4: OPENING THE QUARTERS

In turn, invite the Elemental Guardians into the circle to stand at the four Watchtowers or Quarters. You may like to reread about them in Chapter 3, page 34.

Alternatively, request the presence of the four main archangels: Uriel in the north, Raphael in the east, Michael in the south, and Gabriel in the west.

Greeting the Guardians

Moving around the inside of the perimeter of the cast circle, when you reach the center of the first visualized quadrant, Earth, in the north, face north, raise both arms (palms flat and uppermost), and say: *Wise guardian of the north, hail and welcome.*

Then continue to Air, Fire, and Water, ultimately returning to the altar.

Ask for the qualities of each appropriate elemental power, such as the inspiration of Fire to enter the ritual and perhaps describe the place of fire/light you *see* the Fire Guardian stepping from. Then make the invoking pentagram (see page 8) at each Quarter.

If in a group, everyone faces the direction being opened, raises their arms, and echoes *Hail and welcome.* They then draw the pentagram in the air. Some practitioners make the pentagram *before* the greeting—your choice.

In a group, four different people can lead opening each Quarter.

Using the Pentagram to Greet the Guardians

There are two ways of greeting the Guardians with the pentagram as you face each direction.

Either use the generic invoking pentagram described in Chapter 3 (page 8), which is in fact the Earth element–invoking pentagram (see page 56 for element-specific pentagrams). Alternatively, make a different invoking elemental pentagram according to the element of the Quarter being opened.

To Remind You of the All-Purpose Invoking Pentagram

Pentagrams are generally drawn from chest height with an outstretched and bent arm at about a 60-degree angle to the body. You should be facing outward, toward the Watchtower. The pentagrams should be drawn at the size of a large dinner plate or a small round shield.

Draw pentagrams with your athame, your wand, the index finger and second finger of your power hand together with the rest tucked in, or the whole hand with all fingers together.

If using the different elemental pentagrams to open a Watchtower, draw the pentagram starting from the point *opposite* its elemental point on the pentagram (see the element-specific pentagrams on page 56).

To close the Watchtower at the end of the ritual, draw the pentagram *starting* from its elemental point on the pentagram.

Invoke *toward* and banish *away* from the element you're working with.

Pentagrams are either visualized in their own colors—green for Earth, yellow for Air, red for Fire, and blue for Water—or as a brilliant, electric blue.

The following diagrams will remind you of the elemental positions so you know where to start drawing:

INVOKING EARTH

BANISHING EARTH

INVOKING WATER

BANISHING WATER

Stage 5: Inviting In the Wise Ones

Next, invite chosen ancestors, spiritual and actual, into the circle, plus your spirit guides and guardian angels of those of anyone present.

Face west and either blow a horn, call with your voice, make nine short drum beats, ring the bell nine times, or strike the ground with your staff to invite them in.

If outdoors, swing around in a complete clockwise circle from the north, arms open wide, palms outermost and vertical, asking into the circle any benign fey beings and nature spirits if they wish to attend.

Finally face south, open your arms wide again, and ask if the deities (you can name them) would enter your circle and ritual.

Stage 6: Defining Ceremonially the Purpose of the Ritual

If working alone, begin with *I am* and state your magickal names. Then say: *I come here to this place at this hour to [state the purpose of the rite].*

Make your offerings in the central bowl.

If others are present, each person would in turn add their offering or pass around the bowl.

The person leading the ritual would now bless the offerings dish with the four elemental substances—salt, incense, candle, and sacred water—by passing them over the dish or sprinkling them around the dish.

Now the four sacred tools in turn, first the pentacle, then the tip of the athame, then the tip of the wand, and then the chalice, would be circled over them with appropriate elemental blessings.

Then, holding the offerings dish yourself or passing it around the circle four times, ask all present to endow it, first with an Earth strength or quality, then Air, then Fire, and finally Water.

STAGE 7: THE BODY OF THE RITUAL

The body of the ritual involves charging the offerings with power, in the same way as in spell-casting: dancing, drumming, chanting, etc., with a chosen person leading the group, perhaps in a spiral or circle dance, faster and faster around the altar.

Alternatively, there could be the speaking of the charge (wise words) of the Goddess/God, and then you or whoever spoke them would be moved to speak spontaneously about the purpose of the ritual (see next chapter), with anyone present adding their own inspiration aloud.

STAGE 8: RELEASING THE POWER/THE RESOLUTION

Once the power has been raised, it is released to rise and fall into the offerings symbol. Everyone present could make a final leap, clap, and then sit or stand motionless, allowing the cone power to rise and enter the offerings and all present.

STAGE 9: THE CHALICE AND BLADE RITE

In a personal ritual, this would form the closing part of the ceremony, or among a group, as the cakes/ale part following is an extension of this.

Take the chalice/goblet in your receptive hand and your athame in your power hand and gently lower the tip of the knife so it almost touches the surface of the wine or juice. This represents the joining of Goddess (in the chalice) and God energies (in the knife). Say: *As male to female, God to Goddess, so in this wine/juice is joined in power and love, strength, compassion, striving, and acceptance. Blessed be.*

Pour a little on the ground or indoors in a special bowl to be tipped outdoors later. Now drink a little and leave the rest on the altar or pass/take it around the group for each to drink with a kiss on each cheek and say: *Blessed be.*

STAGE 10: SUBSTITUTING THE CAKES/ALE FOR THE CHALICE/BLADE

This stage adds the element of the Earth/grain to the wine/water (akin to the Christian communion) and is optional.

You need a small cake or biscuit made with honey for each person, plus one as an offering, and a chalice filled with wine or dark-colored fruit juice.

If more than one person is present, one can bless the cakes and two people bless the wine.

Before the ritual, set the cakes toward the north of the altar on a dish or plate marked with a pentacle and the chalice as usual in the west.

At the end of the ritual, raise the cakes skyward in front of the altar as you stand in the south of it facing north.

Lower them to solar plexus level in front of you and make an invoking Earth pentagram, or cross over the cakes with your power hand as you hold them in the other, saying: *May the abundance of the Mother and the bountifulness of the Father bless and nourish, sustain and protect me/you all my/your days. Blessed be.*

Put the plate in the center of the altar.

Take the chalice/goblet in your receptive hand and add the chalice and blade ritual here instead of separately as before.

Afterward, return the chalice to the center of the altar, now to the right of the cakes.

From one of the cakes, scatter a few crumbs on the ground or into an offerings dish if indoors and say: *I return this gift to the Earth Mother in gratitude for blessings received. Blessings be to your mother and to me/all here gathered.*

Now those who did the ritual blessings will each eat a cake and then pass them around to anyone else present. Each recipient says *Blessed be.*

Return the plate to the altar and take the wine, dropping a little on the ground and thanking Mother Earth again for her blessings. Pour this offering into a dish if indoors. You can put the crumbs and liquid outside after the ceremony.

Now drink or offer it to the other person who blessed the chalice. He or she will take a sip and offer it to you or the other person who carried out the blessing, saying *Blessed be.*

If others are present, pass the cup around so each can take a sip, again saying *Blessed be*.

STAGE 11: RETURNING THE ENERGIES

This is a special time before circle closing for personal/group scrying (water in a bowl or the cauldron with lighted candles around it or in a crystal sphere, passed around); sending healing blessings; singing; softly drumming; or making wishes for the future into a candle flame. Alone, it's a good time for inspired writing in your Book of Shadows.

STAGE 12: CLOSING THE QUARTERS

Face south if you invited deity energies, open your arms wide as you did when calling them and thank them, and say: *Hail and farewell. Until we meet again.* Everyone can do this.

Face west and bid any ancestors farewell by banging the staff or ringing the bell as you did to call them and give thanks, saying: *Hail and farewell. Until we meet again.*

Straight afterward go to the western inner perimeter of the circle and close the elemental gateway of Water (some close north to east, as I suggested in Chapter 3, page 36). Try both and see which works for you. Here I give the alternative that has the advantage of ending where you started with the Guardian of the North.

Raise your arms high and wide, with palms flat and uppermost, and bid *Hail and farewell to the Guardians of the West*, thanking them for their protection and strength and adding *Until we meet again*.

Again everyone present faces west and echoes *Hail and farewell*.

Make the appropriate elemental banishing pentagram at each Quarter if you wish, either before or more usually after the farewell, or make the more generic banishing pentagram (refer to page 37) at each Quarter.

Then slowly, in turn, close each gateway, moving counter-clockwise from wherever you started the closing, saying *Hail and farewell. Until we meet again*, until you are back where you started.

Extinguish any directional candles as you go.

Some people close the gateways in the same direction they opened them, clockwise from north, and you can do this straight after bidding the ancestors farewell by moving *deosil*, sunwise, to the north, but counter-clockwise feels better to me.

Stage 13: Uncasting the Circle

Say or chant: *May the circle that is cast forever be unbroken, may the love of the Goddess be forever in my/our heart(s). Merry meet and merry part and merry meet again* (a popular Wiccan chant). Another favorite of mine is: *May I/you never hunger. May I/you never thirst. May I/you never cry alone without loving arms to hold me/you. And may the Goddess hold me/you in the palm of her hand until I/we draw close again.*

Reread the section in Chapter 2 on uncasting circles, page 19.

Stage 14: Afterward

If in a group, often musical offerings or poems are spoken and a bring-and-share meal enjoyed. If alone, have something especially good to eat and drink afterward whilst listening to gentle music.

Leave the altar candles burning till you leave.

In the next chapter, we will work with the Goddesses of Wicca.

THE GODDESS
IN WICCA

THE GODDESS IS CENTRAL TO WICCA AND SOMETIMES IS THE main or sole focus of Wiccan ritual, regarded as giving birth to the world, all people, and creatures, as well as the sun, stars, and moon. Her God/son/consort is considered to be her first creation. So male Wiccans, being part of her creation, possess the Goddess spark and have the Goddess power within them.

Indeed, in modern Wicca, the magickal charge or sacred words of the Goddess—which are attributed to Doreen Valiente, the High Priestess of Gerald Gardner, the founder of Wicca—say: *From Me all things proceed, and unto Me all things must return. Let thine innermost divine self be enfolded in the rapture of the infinite.*

THE MOTHER OF ALL

The Mother of All describes the all-encompassing cosmic force from which all life comes, containing male and female; dark and light; the potential for good and evil; creation and its alter ego, destruction; life and death; and lastly rebirth and renewal.

The first Mother Goddess fertility stone statuettes date back to more than 20,000 years ago, in areas stretching from the Pyrenees to Siberia. The original fertility mothers, who used to invoke the fecundity of humankind and the herds, were pregnant and at first featureless with prominent breasts and hips.

Fertility rituals remained at the heart of the relationship between humans and Mother Earth as they turned to farming, for it was believed that the fertility of the land, the animals, and people were inextricably linked. Making love in the fields at the time of planting was believed to awaken the fertility of the land and the people.

The God also changed from the Horned God to the hunter, still the chief god in Wicca; the god of vegetation; the protector and avenger to farmer, warrior, priest, or king; and grain-sacrifice god.

THE SACRED MARRIAGE

The separated God and Goddess powers are at the roots of Wicca as they have been in magick since Neolithic times. Some covens and magical practitioners use sex magick between committed couples in private with the moment of mutual orgasm acting as the trigger for the release of magick power. However, the sacred marriage is usually, as I described in the previous chapter, symbolized by plunging an athame or ritual knife, which signifies the male generative power, into the receptive chalice of blessed water and wine, or the waters of the womb. I have written more about the Sacred Marriage in the next chapter on the God in Wicca.

ASSUMING GODDESS POWERS MAGICKALLY, STRENGTHENING THE GODDESS WITHIN

In Ancient Egypt, it was believed that speaking as though you were a deity would amplify the higher deity power within yourself, because we all contain the spark of the Goddess creation and are a part of her. The charge or sacred words of the Goddess have become a part of Wiccan tradition.

THE CHARGE OF THE GODDESS

In modern magick, calling down the Goddess power has been incorporated in a formal ceremony called the charge of the Goddess. This is often performed on the night of the full moon, at the *esbat*, as part of Drawing Down the Moon. It is said to induce a trance whereby the Goddess can speak through you. Indeed, it can form part of any ritual or private meditation, whether you are working alone, as part of a group, or in a formal coven.

Creating Your Own Goddess Charge

The charge of the Goddess acts as the vehicle for the Goddess power so that you speak inspired words as though you are the Goddess. You may find that even carefully learned or crafted words change as you link with the Goddess power psychically, so your personal charge will evolve over time.

In the tradition of Gerald Gardner, Doreen Valiente, a very gifted witch, worked to create a beautiful charge of the Goddess for use in a coven. There are also other versions of the charges online. The original charge was spoken through the form of the Moon Goddess Diana and recorded in the book *Aradia, or the Gospel of the Witches*. It is said that anthropologist Charles Leland was given the original manuscript from an Italian witch named Maddalena in the late 1890s.

However, I do believe that it can be helpful even if you are practicing formal coven witchcraft to create your own private or joint coven version of the Charge of the Goddess.

Initially, work around the basic framework I suggest on the following pages or an online version. Make sure to keep a recorder running.

Listen to the recording afterward but do not attempt to rewrite it word for word. Rather use the words as personal or group inspiration with one person as a scribe.

Keep your charge relatively short so you can memorize it fairly easily. Now you can make it part of your personal Goddess rituals and recite it during full moons.

The Stages of the Charge

STAGE 1: THE MOTHER IN ALL HER ASPECTS

This opening section refers to the Mother of All, the single generative creative force that contains male and female, darkness and light, creation and destruction, and birth and rebirth.

I am the Great Mother who has been known in many forms and by many names in countless ages, yet I am and always will be one and the same, your protective and loving Mother. I created you and so I am within you and you in me so do not fear, but love and respect me and so revere yourself.

STAGE 2: THE GODDESS DEFINES HERSELF IN YOUR LIFE AS THE FEMALE QUEEN OF THE EARTH AND HEAVENS

Continue speaking as if you were the Goddess. This is a section where you can add the names of any goddesses listed in this chapter, online, or in books. The form of Ancient Egyptian Isis—a predominant Wiccan Goddess—is often called the Goddess of 10,000 names; a reminder that all Goddesses (and Gods) are aspects of one energy.

When the moon is full or at any time of the day or night, in any season, and whenever you are in need of my help, wisdom, or comfort, find a quiet place and call me into your life to reawaken my presence within you. I am not only your Mother, but also your sister, friend, daughter, and grandmother.

Bring me your hopes with the growing moon and share your dreams as the moon is full, and I will help you make them happen. Let me carry away your sorrows and fears, as the moon dies each month. For I am with you in your youth and your age, whenever you call.

I am in the moon as she passes through the sky, in the brilliant sun chariot of noon, in the fertile earth and the mighty waters and in the stars. You likewise are the moon, sun, fertile earth, the waters, the stars, the four winds, and the life-giving rain, and, like them, and like me, are you eternal.

STAGE 3: THE GIFTS OF THE GODDESS

This section focuses on the gifts the Goddess brings.

I come to you in love as a gentle mother. I can be fierce in defense of you, my young, yet demanding always the greatest good and the purest of words, thoughts, and deeds from you, my precious children. As I give life, so in death all return to me to be transformed, renewed, and born again. I was with you in the beginning and will be with you in the end, holding your hand as you move into renewed light.

STAGE 4: THE RESPONSIBILITIES AND BLESSINGS OF SEEKING A CONNECTION WITH THE GODDESS

This section talks about continuing the Goddess connection through awakening and developing your own spark, core, or divinity.

If you always work magickally with honor, love, and humility, and for the highest good, you carry within you my power and blessings to heal others. So build what is of lasting worth and spread light and goodness throughout the earth. For what you give willingly to those in need, I will restore to you three times three and more, through all time, forevermore.

We are of the circle, and we are the circle. May the circle, cast in my name, live forever in your hearts and in your lives, without beginning and without ending, like my love.

Blessed be.

MOON GODDESS POWER

Though in more formal rituals Drawing Down the Moon is based around the Charge of the Goddess, this simplified version can be used effectively alone, with friends or in your coven during a full moon.

You could begin with a circle-casting and the charge spoken by one person while others softly sway and absorb the words and the wisdom spoken by the High Priestess or ritual leader. Once the charge is completed, it can be followed with inspired words by everyone.

You will need water in a cauldron or a large clear glass bowl and silver bells on a small hoop or string for each person.

Set the bowl or cauldron in front of you as you face the moon or in the center of a group of people or a coven.

Hold bells in your receptive hand.

Stand in full moonlight looking up at the moon. For your first time drawing down the moon, try it when the moon is shining brightly. When you are more experienced, you can visualize the brilliant moon rays even if it is very cloudy. You can also use silver candles around the bowl.

If more than one person is present, stand in a circle with enough space between you to spin around separately.

Raise your arms wide and high, palms uppermost and slightly curved (some people hold them flat).

Call the Moon Mother with a chant, such as: *Draw down the Moon, draw down the power, Mother Great Mother, at this hour. Draw down the Moon, draw down the power, Selene* (Sell-ee-nee), *Diana, Isis, Hecate,* (Hekartay or Heck-at-ay), *Cerridwen, Mothers of the Moon. Come to me. Fill me with light and life, Mothers of the Moon.*

Dance around the water, chanting and spiraling in moonwise, *widdershins*, or counter-clockwise circles as you go, moving your bells rhythmically.

When you are spinning fast, stop and turn around in small moonwise circles, still chanting. This works whether you are alone or with others.

Circle your arms as you move in front of you, over and around your body, chanting faster and moving faster until you become dizzy.

With a final call of *Come within me. Be with me, Mothers of the Moon*, sink to the ground, look up, and the physical moon will come rushing toward you. This is purely psychological, but it is the most effective psychic method I know for bringing together the experience on all levels.

If alone, you may spontaneously speak or sing aloud or hear words channeled from the Moon Mother.

In a formal coven, the High Priestess may initially channel the Moon Goddess energy.

Use the absorbed rush of power to direct a wish or send healing by pointing with both hands and fingers outstretched in the direction from which fulfillment will come or toward the direction that healing will be sent.

When you are ready, gaze into your bowl of water into which the moon is shining and images will enter your mind. If it is a cloudy night, light tiny silver candles around the bowl.

If working with others, each of you should draw close to the water in a tight circle, kneeling or sitting. You can pass the bowl around the group and each person can speak a few words or describe images as the Moon Mother speaks to you.

Unless the weather is bad remain in the moonlight, singing, dreaming, or working with your tarot cards. You can also create an inspired moon chant in your Book of Shadows.

Leave the water out overnight in the moonlight, which can then be used for healing and anointing, and in other rituals as the Water element or as a blessing in the month ahead.

In the next chapter, we will explore the role of the God in Wicca and his charge, and base a ritual around the sacred union of God and Goddess power.

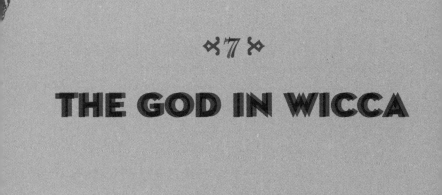

❖ 7 ❖

THE GOD IN WICCA

IN MANY WICCAN TRADITIONS, THE GODDESS REMAINS SUPREME and more powerful than the God, which originates from her.

However, though the Goddess retains her greater role as the first and ultimate Creator, she also offers more specific anima or yin aspects that form the alter ego and balance to the God energies.

In witchcraft, there is a huge range of deity focuses from many ages and cultures so that we can connect with different gods and goddesses. This is so we can connect with the ones that are right for us ritually and personally. Of course, you do not need to remain within a single culture for your Goddess/God pairing.

As you learn more about the gods and goddesses from your own research and rituals, write down their special qualities in your Book of Shadows. This way you can mix and match deity qualities in your pairings, remembering all gods are one God and all goddesses have different features of the same Goddess power.

CREATING AND USING THE GOD CHARGE

You will find charges of the God in Wiccan literature, but you can create your own in exactly the same way as you did for the Goddess.

If you are working alone, try creating your charge while sitting in the bright sunlight. The charge is linked with bringing down the power of the Sun God at mid-summer, dawn, noon, or during rituals where you want to draw down the God power for strength or courage. You can recite the God charge at your altar or outdoors in sunlight to absorb and bring forth your inner God energy.

In a group, pass a wand or athame from person to person, stating what God power means to you.

If alone, gaze into a clear crystal sphere and you will see many images of power and glory that can inspire you to follow your dreams.

Once created, different people can create and recite different parts of the whole charge during ceremonies. Or one person such as a designated High Priest can speak while others visualize the God and draw his power within them.

A RITUAL TO HEAL THROUGH THE SYMBOLIC SACRED MARRIAGE

Drawing Down the Moon can be added to this ritual and into any other ritual as well. You can carry it out alone or in a group.

Prepare the altar, cast a circle in the usual way, and open the Watchtowers.

Light the Goddess candle and the God candle using the flame

from the Goddess candle, saying *As one becomes two, may blessings increase and light grow.*

Hold a frankincense or sandalwood incense stick first in the Goddess candle flame and then in the God candle flame, saying *As one becomes two, may blessings increase and power grow.*

Take your athame or wand, raising it toward the sky, sun, or moon at a 60-degree angle.

You, or everyone present, raise the athame and say *By seed and root, by stem and bud, by leaf and flower and fruit, I call you God and Goddess [name chosen deities].*

Next, if working alone, touch the center of your forehead with the blade or wand, directing it toward your feet and saying *Blessed be the feet that walk within your paths of light.*

Direct it toward your knees and say *Blessed be the knees that kneel upon the silver earth in praise.*

Direct the athame toward your womb, or, for a male witch, the genitals, and say *Blessed be the womb/the source of procreation that ever renews and generates new life.*

Next, direct the athame toward the heart, saying *Blessed be the heart of love, beauty, and strength.*

Finally, touch your lips gently with the blade or wand, saying *Blessed be the lips that speak words of mystery and of truth Divine.*

However, if in a group, form a circle around the Goddess designate and direct your blades toward her as you all speak the words. The Goddess designate will remain silent, standing with her athame or wand pointing directly upward to the sun, moon, or sky while the God designate gently touches her body with the wand or blade.

If working alone, stand and raise the athame again toward the sun, moon, or sky and say *By seed and root, by stem and bud, by leaf and flower and fruit, by Life and Love, do I call you gracious Goddess and God. Fill me with your blessings and your wisdom.*

If in a group, again direct your blade or wand toward the figures in the center and speak the chant together, adapting the words. Again, the Goddess figure remains silent with her athame or wand raised toward the moon, sun, or sky.

If alone, now lower your blade and stand with your body, legs, and arms apart with your arms raised.

If you are in a group, the Goddess designate now speaks the charge of the Goddess by moonlight, or the designated High Priest speaks the God charge if working in daylight or as dawn breaks, while the others sway softly. Speak the appropriate charge if alone. The group would point their athame or wand toward the Goddess and God as they speak.

The moon would not be drawn down by spinning but by you or the group each holding the wand or athame toward the moon and allowing the moon power to enter each person as you listen to the Goddess charge or by saying it if you're alone.

Now the God designate takes up the blade or wand from the altar where the Goddess designate put it. She holds the chalice and says *Who does the blade serve?* He raises the blade above the chalice and says *You, my Goddess, forevermore and all who need its power and protection.*

She raises the chalice so that the point of the blade is almost touching the liquid inside and he asks *Whom does the Grail cup heal?*

She answers *You, my God, forevermore and all who seek its love and its fertility.*

Now he lifts the chalice over the Goddess candle and says *From the womb of the Mother.*

The Goddess passes the blade through the incense smoke and says *And the seed of the Father.*

He plunges the knife into the chalice or glass and says *Comes the unity of creation. So may God and Goddess ever be united and may the purpose of this rite be granted in the unity of love and healing.*

Take both parts if alone.

Then the chalice is passed around after the Goddess designate has offered it to the God designate and the God to the Goddess, and she pours a little on the ground.

After this, all may speak and ask or make blessings.

When you are ready, close your Watchtowers, uncast your circle, and blow out the candles.

In the next chapter, we will study the all-important Wheel of the Year—the eight seasonal change points that are central to Wiccan rituals.

THE WHEEL OF THE YEAR IN WICCA

THE WHEEL OF THE YEAR HAS EIGHT DIVISIONS THAT ARE central to Wicca, splitting the year approximately into six-week periods.

THE SIGNIFICANCE OF THE EIGHTFOLD YEAR

Some witches in the southern hemisphere move everything around six month—for example, celebrating the Mid-Summer Solstice on or around December 21.

THE STRUCTURE OF THE WHEEL

The four Solar festivals, the Quarter Days, the Lesser Sabbats, the Equinoxes, and the Solstices that fall midpoint through the four seasons vary date-wise each year by a day or two because of the tilt of the earth.

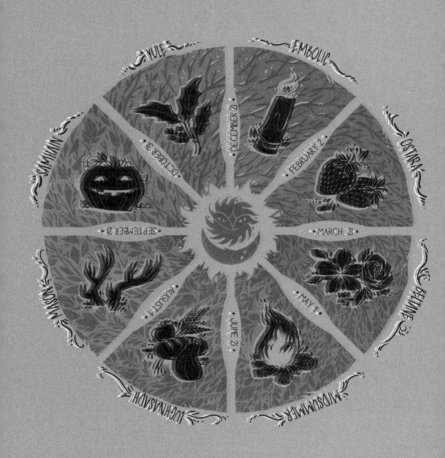

Magickally, they are celebrated like the other four points on the Wheel—from sunset the evening before, the beginning of the Celtic day, until sunset on the day, after the festival day, giving a forty-eight-hour period for each.

The Cross-Quarter Days, which fall midway between each of these Solar festivals, are four Fire festivals that form major rites in the Wiccan calendar. Create your own ritual celebrations, whether alone, in a coven, or with family and friends.

The four Greater Sabbats are sometimes calculated as the day upon which the sun enters fifteen degrees of Scorpio for Samhain (end of October or the beginning of November), fifteen degrees of Aquarius for Oimelc (end of January or the beginning of February), fifteen degrees of Taurus for Beltane (end of April or the beginning of May), and fifteen degrees of Leo for Lughnasadh (end of July or the beginning of August).

For every festival, in your Book of Shadows write the ongoing story of your personal Wheel and your plans when the Wheel reaches this point again in twelve months' time.

THE FESTIVALS

Weave your own celebrations small or large, alone or with others, using the appropriate candle colors. With a large group, have a big central offerings bowl or cauldron.

Imbolc (Imbolg) or Oimelc

Dates: January 31–February 2

Type of Day: Cross-Quarter

Focus: New ideas, planning the future, new love and trust, the first steps to launch new projects, melting conflicts, newborn infants, babies, and young animals

Direction: Northeast

Place on the Wheel: *Oimelc* is named after the first ewe's milk available after winter. *Imbolc* means fire in the belly and is the awakening of passion in the Maiden Goddess.

Alban Eiler, Ostara, or the Spring Equinox
Dates: March 20–March 22

Type of Day: Quarter

Focus: Fertility and positive life changes, new beginnings and opportunities, flowering love, ventures, travel, moving, clearing what is no longer needed in your life, conception, pregnancy, children, and young people

Direction: East

Place on the Wheel: *Alban Eiler* means in Gaelic "the Light of the Earth that returns after the winter from the Otherworld." Ostara is the Norse goddess of spring.

Beltane or Beltaine
Dates: April 30–May 2

Type of Day: Cross-Quarter; the secondmost important of the year and the beginning of Celtic summer

Focus: For people in their twenties and thirties, fertility, increasing commitment in love, consummation of love, creativity, improving health, and abundance

Direction: Southeast

Place on the Wheel: Named after the Gallic fire and sun god Bel, Belenus, Belinus, or Belenos, or the earlier Gallic solar and fire goddess Belissima.

Alban Heruin, Litha, Mid-Summer or Summer Solstice
Dates: June 20–22

Type of Day: Major Quarter

Focus: Power, joy and courage, male potency, success, marriage, people approaching middle age, happiness, wealth, and career opportunities

Direction: South

Place on the Wheel: *Litha* means light, and Alban Heruin is the light of the shore as the sun floods over the land, ripening the crops (the longest day of the year). The first light on Solstice morn acts as a shaft of gold across standing stones and stone circles, linking the dimensions.

Lughnasadh/Lammas
Dates: July 31–August 2

Type of Day: Cross-Quarter

Focus: People in their forties and fifties, justice, human rights, partnerships, personal and business relationships, contracts or property matters, willing to sacrifice for the greater good

Direction: Southwest

Place on the Wheel: Named after the Irish sun god Lugh, he renews the Sacred Marriage with Eriu/Nass, the Irish Earth Goddess, transferring his remaining light to her for the continuing growth of the crops.

Alban Elued, Mabon, Autumn Equinox

Dates: September 21–23

Type of Day: Quarter

Focus: The completion of tasks, fruition of long-term goals, mending quarrels, receiving money owed, financial and material security, all matters concerning retirement and older people, and chronic health problems

Direction: West

Place on the Wheel: In Gaelic, *Alban Elued* means light on the water. The sun is moving away over the water to shine on the Isles of the Blest. In traditional celebrations, a priestess distributes wheat, fruit, and vegetables.

Samhain

Dates: October 31–November 2

Type of Day: Major Cross-Quarter; most important of the year and the beginning of the Celtic winter and New Year

Focus: For people in their seventies and eighties, family ancestors, looking into the past and the future, protection, psychic and physical, overcoming fears of aging and mortality, and for retired people

Direction: Northwest

Place on the Wheel: Another fire festival, Samhain means summer's end, the time when the herds were brought down from the hills and family members including the ancestors returned to the homestead for the winter.

Alban Arthuran, Yule, or Mid-Winter Solstice

Dates: December 20–February 22

Type of Day: Major Quarter

Focus: The rebirth of light and hope, domestic happiness and security, family togetherness, home and property, accepting what cannot be changed, for very old people, carers, and welcoming home the absent

Direction: North

Place on the Wheel: *Alban Arthuran* means in Gaelic the light of Arthur and refers to the rebirth of Arthur, the Sun King in myth, as the Divine Child. At this time, people held feasts as a magickal gesture to attract abundance.

In the next chapter I will describe how best to work as a solitary practitioner, set up a coven, or join an existing coven.

FORMING OR JOINING A COVEN OR WORKING SOLO

WORKING MAGICKALLY WITH OTHERS

COVEN IS THE NAME GIVEN TO A REGULAR GATHERING OF Wiccan practitioners, formally organized under the direction of a High Priestess, who may have been trained in a particular Wiccan tradition.

Within a formal coven, initiation after a year and a day or a similar recognized magickal period will confer formal entry into the coven. After another one to two years, they can elevate to a second or third degree of Wicca, so that eventually initiates can begin their own covens if they wish.

There will usually be an initiated High Priestess, sometimes a maiden who assists the High Priestess, and a crone, who is a wise woman experienced in witchcraft. The traditional thirteen members are linked to the thirteen moons during the years, and thirteen is also the number of the Goddess.

However, many people organize a magickal group that follows Wiccan principles but is much less formal, where members will adopt different roles according to their own talents and interests. Online covens are also springing up, and they are an excellent way for solitary practitioners to gain support and information.

SOLITARY WITCHCRAFT

Many witches such as myself choose to practice alone, drawing in family and close friends on seasonal festivals. Most initiate themselves. Though solitary Wiccans use ceremonial magick, many follow less formal folk magick. For this reason, some are styled hedgewitches, which refers to the times when a hedge, especially a hawthorn, was bound to the witch's home to repel curious people. This title also refers to the ability of the witch to walk through astral projection on the hedge between the worlds.

HOW TO FIND A COVEN

Formal covens are in short supply, but with persistence, you will find the right one. Many modern covens do not practice sky-clad or naked, as this can make some people feel very self-conscious. This would also entail the need for very strong parameters to avoid the ceremony spilling into everyday relationships. Like ritual sex between God and Goddess, modern covens follow a symbolic chalice/blade rite with sacred sex, if at all, carried out in private by an established couple who leave the circle once uncast to avoid any complications.

Of course, you have to be careful, because the hidden nature of witchcraft means it is harder to weed out the charlatans and weirdos. To find the right coven, try entry through pagan organizations and established reputable New Age stores. You can attend properly arranged workshops and celebrations organized by recognized Wiccan organizations. Also, you can talk to people at events, visit healing festivals, buy established and reputable pagan magazines, and take it slow until everything feels right. No reputable coven will advertise for members, ask to meet you in places you consider unsafe, or ask you to do anything that feels uncomfortable.

Nor will a reputable coven be in a hurry to sign you up. In fact, the opposite is true. Avoid offers of signing in blood, being initiated by having sex with the High Priest or High Priestess, or promising to fall on a sword should you leave the coven or betray secrets.

Nor should you pay huge sums of money upfront for training. You'll pay for expenses and for membership of an established pagan/goddess organization, but these organizations tend to ask for remarkably little.

True Wiccans would never seek to impose their beliefs on others and are usually incredibly reticent with people they do not know.

STARTING YOUR OWN INFORMAL COVEN

You can, however, start a less formal coven with friends without subscribing to any particular form of Wicca. Some of the most spiritual Wiccan covens are those that do not have a High Priestess or High Priest role but instead take turns organizing the meetings and rituals.

A wise member may look after newcomers, explain basic rituals, suggest reading material, and guide them through at-home work with meditation and visualization. Certain members may undertake researching aspects of the Craft that interest them or collect information about deities, which can help them run informal sessions.

In establishing your group, have a preliminary meeting to plan ahead, deciding on the topics, venue, and equipment you will need.

Use a good almanac and moon diary relevant to your region. You can arrange to meet on the crescent moon as well as the full moon for a candle-lighting ceremony, where you can make wishes and blessings burned in your own zodiac candle color (described in Chapter 10, page 97), as well as on major seasonal festivals or for special healing work.

Have a joint fund for candles, crystals, incense, and anything else you need. Make sure to appoint one person to check supplies.

Appoint one or two people to organize specific festivals and to act as High Priest/Priestess for that occasion. The most reticent member may prove the most dynamic at singing chants and raising energies.

COVEN TREASURES

Have a box or chest of basic coven tools, such as a central chalice and athame to put on the altar where you hold your meetings (each person will want their own athame and wand as well).

Items such as a silver bell, crystal chalice, or large goblet can be gathered from members' homes. Scarves or throws make for excellent altar cloths. You can make pentacles from clay or beeswax in a group craft session as well as wands from a trip to the forest.

Have two Books of Shadows, one as a permanent record, traditionally copied out by hand by the group scribe, and another ongoing working almanac to which everyone contributes. Also note in the almanac current moon phases for the month and calculate the times of day when particular planets and angels hold sway. If you keep this information ongoing on a computer in a jointly accessible account, you can print out copies for other members.

In the final chapter I will suggest magickal colors, herbs, crystal meanings, and the magickal timings you can use to weave your own rituals and spells.

❖ 10 ❖

MAGICKAL CORRESPONDENCES

THIS CHAPTER OFFERS A RESOURCE BASE FOR CREATING your own spells and rituals that lie at the heart of Wicca. Since each color, fragrance, time of day, moon phase, and even day of the week has its own magickal significance, you can craft precisely the energies you need in your magick by mixing and matching the materials and quantities.

The following are associations that have worked well for me for more than forty years and are based on accepted magickal principles. However, you may come across equally valid alternatives. See what works best for you and through your Book of Shadows create the form of Wicca that is right for you.

DIFFERENT KINDS OF MAGICK

Attracting or Sympathetic Magick

Add a coin to a pot daily to encourage the steady accumulation of material resources, or keep a tiny doll in a cradle next to your bed in order to help you conceive. *Deosil* (clockwise) movements signify attracting energies.

Banishing Magick

Banishing magick removes or returns any negativity, psychic attacks, or physical threats to you, your home, or loved ones and takes away bad habits and fears. Light a candle, tie a knot in a strong thread, and hold the knot in the candle flame. When it breaks, say *I cut the ties that bind me,* blow out the candle, and bury the thread in soil. Banishing magick generally involves *widdershins* (anti-clockwise) movements.

Binding Magick

Bind a person from harming you or your loved ones by making a featureless clay image of the perpetrator, tie the figure with knotted thread or a ribbon, and declare what behavior is to be bound. Then wrap the figure in soft cloth, and put it in a closed drawer until the problem resolves or the figure crumbles. Alternatively, write the name of the perpetrator in red ink on a piece of paper, put a cross through the name, and keep it for three months in the coldest part of your freezer.

Candle Magick

Engrave an unlit candle with your astrological glyph, words, names, or wishes, using a paper knife. Or you can invisibly draw symbols on the wax with your index finger of your dominant hand. Then light the candle, releasing the power of the message or zodiac sign as the wax melts and banishes what you wish to remove from your life by allowing the candle to burn and then extinguishing it, saying *May [what you wish to remove] be gone with the dimming of this light*.

Astrological Symbols and Candle Magick

Etch the glyph of the current zodiac period or any zodiac period at any time in the year whose energies you need on a candle. For example, etch the Leo glyph on a gold-colored candle for leadership or fame. The power is strongest during your own birth sign period.

Aries

THE RAM | MARCH 21–APRIL 20 | RED

For all matters of self and identity, innovation, assertiveness, courage, and action.

Taurus

THE BULL | APRIL 21–MAY 21 | PINK OR GREEN

For beauty, harmony, all material matters and security, for patience, and persistence.

Gemini

THE HEAVENLY TWINS | MAY 22–JUNE 21 | YELLOW OR PALE GRAY

For communication, learning, choices, versatility, short-distance travel, and speculation.

Cancer

THE CRAB | JUNE 22–JULY 22 | SILVER

For home and family, fertility, mothering, protection, gentle love, friendship, and wishes.

Leo

THE LION | JULY 23–AUGUST 23 | GOLD

For fame and fortune, leadership, sensual pleasures, the arts, and love affairs.

Virgo

THE MAIDEN | AUGUST 24–SEPTEMBER 22 | GREEN

For efficiency, bringing order to chaos, self-improvement, attention to detail, health, and healing.

Libra

THE SCALES | SEPTEMBER 23–OCTOBER 23 | BLUE

For justice and the law, balancing options and priorities, harmony and reconciliation, and charisma.

Scorpio

THE SCORPION | OCTOBER 24–NOVEMBER 22 | INDIGO OR BURGUNDY

For increasing second sight, passion and sex, keeping secrets, burning ambition, and claiming what is rightfully yours in any area of life.

Sagittarius

THE ARCHER | NOVEMBER 23–DECEMBER 21 | ORANGE OR TURQUOISE

For optimism, fresh perspectives, long-distance travel and moving, creative ventures, and expanding horizons.

Capricorn

THE GOAT | DECEMBER 22–JANUARY 20 | BROWN OR BLACK

For wise caution, achieving ambitions through perseverance, authority, loyalty, acquisition and preservation of money and property.

Aquarius

THE WATER CARRIER | JANUARY 21–FEBRUARY 18 | PURPLE OR DARK BLUE

For independence, friendship, ingenuity, original perspectives, detachment from emotional pressures, and altruism.

Pisces

THE FISH | FEBRUARY 19–MARCH 20 | SOFT WHITE OR MAUVE

For increased spiritual awareness and intuition, imagination, spiritual gifts, and fulfilling hidden dreams.

Knot Magick

A series of three, seven, or nine knots tied can be used for attracting magick where each knot is empowered by words said while tying it. The knots act as a storage cell for energies that can be released by untying one knot every day. For love use a red knot cord to tie two images together face-to-face.

Weather Magick

Use rain to wash away words of loss or pain written in chalk outdoors. Use wind to blow free paper wish messages tied to a tree on a hill or dying leaves on a dead branch, each named for a sorrow.

Colors

Colors can be used magickally with candles, flowers, and crystals. You can even use colored purses containing herbs and crystals.

White for multi-purpose, attracting rituals, and workplace magick.

Red for passion, strength, change, action, and overcoming obstacles.

Orange for happiness, creativity, independence, and fertility.

Yellow for anti-spite, short-term travel and moving, learning new things, speculation, loans, credit, and business.

Green for commitment in love, twin souls, good luck, environment, beauty, and harmony.

Blue for leadership, justice, career, marriage, riches, long-term or long-distance travel, moving, interviews, and tests.

Purple for spiritual development, healing, psychic protection, imaginative ventures, anti-addiction, and overcoming fears and phobias.

Pink for reconciliation, children, healing of abuse, home, and family.

Brown for property and DIY, official organizations, banks and finances, animals, accumulation of resources, stability, and for older people.

Silver for intuition and hidden potential; fertility; sea, moon, and star magick; and slow-growing prosperity.

Gold for fame and fortune, aiming high, wishes coming true, major ambitions, all sun magick, and good fortune.

Black for endings, protection against evil, banishing, and binding.

MAGICKAL TOOLS AND MATERIALS

Crystals

Start a personal collection of crystals for magick and healing. Crystals, when worn as jewelry or carried in a small bag, can be used as an amulet of protection or as a lucky talisman to attract a particular result.

Green amazonite protects against others taking advantage, attracts business, money spells, brings good luck when gambling or speculating (as does green aventurine), and anti-bullying against women.

Purple amethyst is known as the All-Healer. It removes negative earth energies from a home, brings balance to people and situations, and is used for older women's power, Wise Woman ceremonies, and anti-addiction.

Orange carnelian protects against fire, accidents, storms, malevolence of all kinds and psychic intrusion, for mature love, sex, and fertility.

Yellow citrine guards against negative people, bad atmospheres, and unfriendly ghosts, and brings prosperity, especially in business. Also, good for ventures, learning new things, travel, and healing.

Clear crystal quartz transforms negativity into rays of light and positivity, calls angels and spirit guides, for any attracting or energizing purpose, and for sun magick. This can be used as a substitute for any other crystal.

Jet stabilizes finances, anti-debt, property matters, protection, for older people, overcoming grief, and psychic invisibility in danger.

Rose Quartz peaceful sleep, heals abuse of any kind, romance, young or new love, fertility, rebuilding of trust, and twin souls (as with green jade).

Sodalite overcomes fears of flying, justice, relocation, tests, examinations, and interviews. This can be used during older women or wise women rituals.

MAGICKAL HERBS, INCENSE, AND OILS

Use herbs in a pouch, or while cooking, and stir the mix or infusions to empower the spell to protect the home, any possessions, your workplace, and property. Use incense in sticks, cones, or as a powder incense and burn it on heated charcoal blocks and use a lighted incense stick like a smoke pen to write empowerments or symbols.

Allspice for money, passion, swift-moving, or urgent matters.

Basil for fidelity, prosperity, protection, and fear of flying.

Chamomile (Roman) and chamomile (German) for healing, babies, children, animals, and reversing bad luck. It also helps to attract money and is helpful in family matters.

Cedar/cedarwood for healing, cleansing bad influences, negative thoughts, and harmony.

Cinnamon for passion, regaining money after loss, urgently needing money, and psychic awareness.

Dragon's blood for fierce protection, anti-curse, any major enterprise, and male potency.

Fennel for travel, house sales, and moves. It helps to banish and keep harm away from people, animals, and places.

Frankincense for wealth, courage, joy, career, success, and travel. Also used in formal rituals.

Hyssop for making a love commitment; healing; spirituality; all forms of protection, especially from psychic attack; and as an infusion to cleanse artifacts.

Juniper purifies homes; protects against accidents, thieves, and illness; and male potency.

Lemongrass/lemon repels spite, malice, and gossip. It also helps with psychic awareness and travel.

Lemon verbena for breaking a run of bad luck, protection against negativity, the Evil Eye, and ill-wishing.

Mint and **peppermint** drives negativity from objects and places, and brings money, health, love, and success.

Myrtle for a lasting marriage, mature love, domestic happiness, property, and security.

Myrrh for healing, peace, purification, overcoming grief, and protection against evil. Can be used in formal rituals and in moon magick.

Pine drives away harm from the home and family, especially newborn infants, cleansing negativity and malice, guarding property, and premises.

Rosemary for learning, love, fidelity, prosperity, and banishing malevolence.

Sage for longevity, good health, examinations, interviews, tests, protection of the home and family, slow-growing prosperity, and wisdom.

Sandalwood for spiritual awareness and healing, leadership, justice, compensation, and sexuality. Can be used in formal rituals.

Tarragon the dragon herb, courage, and anti-bullying, and the shedding of old burdens, guilt, fears, and destructive relationships.

Thyme psychically cleanses the home, possessions, vehicles and land, health, memory of past worlds, and drives away nightmares and phantoms of the night.

Vetivert for love, breaks a run of bad luck, protects against theft and negativity.

MAGICKAL FLOWERS

Use potted flowers, petals, fresh or dried, as potpourri mixes, essential oils, or flower essences.

Geranium heals domestic conflict and trouble in the workplace, for first or new love, and money.

Hyacinth for self-esteem, rebuilding trust after betrayal, domestic happiness, increasing radiance, and attracting beautiful things into your life.

Jasmine for powerful love, sacred sex, and optimism. Used for all moon and night magick.

Lavender for love, especially self-love, fertility, happiness, health, guards against cruelty and spite, reduces anti-stress and addiction, and is all-healing.

Marigold increases positive energies in a room or buildings, protects during the night and in domestic matters, for resolution of legal problems and justice, increase of love and commitment.

Rose is the ultimate gentle flower of love and reconciliation. Used for self-esteem; healing the young, the very old, and anyone who has suffered abuse; attracting money; and used in fertility magick. Pink is for new love, red for commitment, yellow for love in later years, and white for secret love.

MAGICKAL TIMES

Where possible, time your spells and rituals so they flow with the prevailing energies.

The Moon

THE WAXING MOON

From day three or four in the monthly moon cycle, when you see the crescent moon in the sky until the night before the full moon. The closer to the full moon, the more intense the energies.

Used magickally for attracting or increasing anything from love to prosperity.

The Full Moon

The day of the full moon represents full power, but also instability. Astrologically, the moon is in opposition (or in the opposite side of the sky) to the sun. The night of a full moon is also called the night of *esbat*.

Used magickally for urgent needs, power, changing luck, fertility, and justice.

The Waning Moon

From the day after the full moon until the waning moon crescent disappears.

Used magickally for banishing what is no longer wanted, such as pain, negative people, and situations.

The New Moon, also called the Dark of the Moon

The new moon appears three days after the waning moon and before the new crescent moon appears in the sky.

Used magickally for binding others from harm, secrets, removing bad habits, and for transformation.

The Sun

There are four main sun times used in spell-casting and rituals. Sun magick is faster and more intense than moon magick, and is used for rapidly moving and ongoing matters.

Dawn

The time of dawn varies each day.

Used magickally for new beginnings, initiating projects, improving health, career prospects, and bringing good fortune.

Dawn represents the east and the spring season in the northern hemisphere.

Noon

Similar to the full moon energy, but more instantaneous and concentrated.

Used magickally for a sudden burst of power, confidence, strength, passion, a fast or urgent infusion of money, and sending absent healing for serious or acute conditions.

Noon represents the south and the summer season in the northern hemisphere.

Dusk

The time of dusk also varies from day to day.

Used magickally for letting go of regrets, anger, or sorrow, and reducing pain, illness, and debt.

Dusk represents the west and the autumn season in the northern hemisphere.

Midnight

Corresponds with the beginning of a new day, but its energies last until dawn.

Used magickally for endings leading to beginnings, contacting wise ancestors, binding and banishing of all kinds, psychic protection, and reversing curses.

Midnight represents the north and the winter season in the northern hemisphere.

The Planets and the Days of the Week

Each of the planets rules a day of the week. Use its associated metals, crystals, incense, and other elements to strengthen a spell or ritual worked on that day.

In addition, the associations with the sun can be used not only on Sunday but with all sun magick, and the Monday associations can be used in all magick.

If you are calling a particular archangel, apply the associations of its planet or weekday.

Days of the Week

SUNDAY

Planet: Sun

Archangel: Michael

Color(s): Gold

Element: Fire

Crystals: Amber, carnelian, diamond, clear crystal quartz, tigereye, or golden topaz

Incense: Cloves, cinnamon, or frankincense

Trees: Bay, birch, or laurel

Herbs and Oils: Chamomile, juniper, rosemary, saffron, or St. John's wort

Metal: Gold

Astrological Rulership: Leo

For ambition, power, and success; for fathers; improving health; prosperity; self-confidence; and overcoming bad luck.

MONDAY

☽

Planet: Moon

Archangel: Gabriel

Color(s): Silver or translucent white

Element: Water

Crystals: Moonstone, mother of pearl, pearl, selenite, or opal

Incense: Jasmine, myrrh, mimosa, or lemon

Trees: Willow or alder

Herbs and Oils: Lotus, poppy, or wintergreen

Metal: Silver

Astrological Rulership: Cancer

For home and family matters, for women (especially mothers and grandmothers), children, animals, fertility, secrets, and psychic gifts.

TUESDAY

♂

Planet: Mars

Archangel: Samael or Camael

Color(s): Red

Element: Fire

Crystals: Garnet, bloodstone, ruby, or red jasper

Incense: Dragon's blood, all spices, ginger, mint, or thyme

Trees: Cypress, holly, or pine

Herbs and Oils: Basil, cinnamon, coriander, garlic, pepper, or tarragon

Metal: Iron or steel

Astrological Rulership: Aries (co-ruler of Scorpio)

For courage, change, independence, overcoming seemingly impossible odds and bullies, energy, passion, strength, perfection, principles, and fierce defense of the vulnerable.

WEDNESDAY

Planet: Mercury

Archangel: Raphael

Color(s): Yellow

Element: Air

Crystals: Yellow agate, citrine, falcon's eye, yellow jasper, malachite, or onyx

Incense: Lavender, lemongrass, or mace

Trees: Hazel or ash

Herbs and Oils: Dill, fennel, parsley, or valerian

Astrological Rulership: Gemini or Virgo

For money making, examinations and tests, learning new things, short-distance travel, moving, short holidays, repelling envy, malice, spite, and deceit.

THURSDAY

♃

Planet: Jupiter

Archangel: Sachiel

Color(s): Blue or purple

Element: Air

Crystals: Azurite, lapis lazuli, sodalite, or turquoise

Incense: Agrimony, cedar, sandalwood, or sage

Tree: Beech, oak, or ash

Herbs and Oils: Borage, cinquefoil, coltsfoot, hyssop, or mistletoe

Metal: Tin

Astrological Rulership: Sagittarius (co-ruler of Pisces)

For expansion, career, leadership, long distance travel, moving, justice, marriage, self-employment, loyalty, male potency, and banishing excesses.

FRIDAY

Planet: Venus

Archangel: Anael

Color(s): Green or pink

Element: Earth

Crystals: Amethyst (also mercury), emerald, jade, moss agate, or rose quartz

Incense: Geranium, rose, strawberry, or vervain

Trees: Almond, apple, or birch

Herbs and Oils: Feverfew, mugwort, pennyroyal, verbena, or yarrow

Metal: Copper

Astrological Rulership: Taurus or Libra

For all love magick, fidelity, sacred sex, mending quarrels, environment, fertility, women's health, gradual growth in all matters, beauty, friendship, reducing the influence of destructive lovers, and possessiveness.

SATURDAY

♄

Planet: Saturn

Archangel: Cassiel

Color(s): Brown, black, or grey

Element: Earth

Crystals: Haematite, jet, lodestone, obsidian, or smoky quartz

Incense: Aconite, cypress, or patchouli

Trees: Blackthorn or yew

Herbs: Aspen, bistort, comfrey, horsetail, or Solomon's seal

Metals: Lead and pewter

Astrological Rulership: Capricorn (co-ruler of Aquarius)

For unfinished business, endings, slow-moving official matters, locating lost objects, animals, anti-addiction and debt, lifting depression, pain and illness, long-term psychic protection, locating lost objects (as well as animals and people), and establishing boundaries.